Your Child at Play: Three to Five Years

Also by the authors:

Your Child At Play: Birth to One Year
Your Child At Play: One to Two Years
Your Child At Play: Two to Three Years
Making Friends
Play Together Grow Together
All About Child Care
Just Pretending

Your Child at Play: Three to Five Years

Marilyn M. Segal, Ph.D.
and
Don Adcock, Ph.D.

Newmarket Press
New York

We would like to thank the A. L. Mailman Family Foundation for its generous support of the research for Your Child At Play.

First Edition
1 2 3 4 5 6 7 8 9 0 (cloth)
1 2 3 4 5 6 7 8 9 0 (paper)

Library of Congress Cataloging-in-Publication Data
Segal, Marilyn M.
   Your child at play
   Bibliography: p.
   Includes index.
   1. Play—United States.   2. Child development.
I. Adcock, Don. II. Title.
HQ782.S426 1986   155.4'18   86-60294
ISBN 0-937858-72-2
ISBN 0-937858-73-0 (pbk.)

LC:86-60294

Volumes in the *Your Child at Play* series:
Your Child at Play: Birth to One Year
Your Child at Play: One to Two Years
Your Child at Play: Two to Three Years
Your Child at Play: Three to Five Years
Published simultaneously in hardcover and paperback editions

Quantity Purchases
Companies, professional groups, clubs, and other organizations may qualify for special terms when ordering quantities of this title. For information, contact the Special Sales Department, Newmarket Press, 18 East 48th Street, New York, New York 10017. Phone (212) 832-3575.

Manufactured in the United States of America

To Amelia, Kori, Jennifer, Brenan, Kenneth, Nicholas, Rachel, Gregory, and Peter who are always there to update our knowledge of child play.

CONTENTS

INTRODUCTION

Rachel, a three-year-old, had a friend over for the afternoon. As usual, Rachel was bossing her friend around and insisting that things be done her way. Rachel's father decided to intervene. "I want you to *behave*," he told her firmly. "I am being 'haive,'" Rachel countered, and continued to bully her friend.

Like Rachel, children from three to five are taking charge of their own play. Whether they are assigning a task to a peer, investigating the properties of mud and water, or staging a safari in the living room, their play is self-initiated and all engaging. The purpose of play is to have a good time. The outcome of play is physical, intellectual, and social development.

Your Child at Play is a description of the play behavior of preschool children. It is based on a three-year observational study of children at play in a variety of settings. Its purpose is to identify and discuss the group commonalities and individual differences in the play of young children and to describe ways in which parents can foster their child's development by supporting their play ideas.

Your Child at Play is divided into five sections, each focused on a different type of play.

Section One, "Conversational Play," describes the ways in which children play with important ideas as they flood their parents with questions.

Section Two, "Discovery Play," describes ways in which children use their play to explore the different properties of living and nonliving things.

Section Three, "Creative Play," views the child as artist, builder, playwright, and storyteller and describes the creative products that are generated through play.

Section Four, "Playing with Letters and Numbers," describes ways in which children teach themselves counting, letter writing, letter and word naming, and other academic skills.

Section Five, "Playing with Friends," describes ways in which children learn to initiate, explore, and maintain early friendships.

For the sake of organization, we have divided different kinds of play into separate categories. However, play seldom falls neatly into one of our categories. When two children sit at the beach shoveling sand for their castle, they are simultaneously engaged in discovery play, creative play, and play with a friend. When a four-year-old playing school teaches an imaginary friend how to count, she is engaged in both creative play and play with letters and numbers.

Because a major purpose of *Your Child at Play* is to help parents understand, enjoy, and contribute to their children's play, a section entitled "Suggestions for Parents" is included in every chapter. In this section, we list play ideas and strategies that have been successfully used by other parents.

We do not suggest that *Your Child at Play* be read as a textbook from cover to cover. Turn to the Contents and begin with a section that describes the kind of play in which your child is most involved. When you reach the suggestions at the end of the chapters, look for play ideas that you and your child might enjoy. Take into account your own interests as well as the interests of your child. Remember that fun is contagious. Sharing a good time with your child is both your responsibility and your reward.

Part I
CONVERSATIONAL PLAY

Rachel, a talkative and curious three-year-old never stops asking questions. "Sometimes they're silly. Sometimes they're easy, and sometimes they're questions that even I can't answer," explained her older sister, Jennifer. Here is the list of questions that Jennifer compiled:

Why do fairies have funny ears?

How do tigers go roar?

Why does your mouth go up when you smile?

What is it going to do in the world today?

Why are we people?

Preschool children like Rachel are so full of questions that we sometimes find ourselves ignoring them. Yet if we tune into their questions, we can recapture the wonderment of things we otherwise take for granted and recall the naive faith that all questions can be answered. At the same time, we can recognize that questions provide a beautiful opportunity to join in the private world of our children:

Rachel: Why do fairies have funny ears?

Mother: Those kind of ears are very good for listening to butterfly talk.

Part I is divided into three chapters. In the first chapter, "Matters of Life and Death," we look at the kinds of questions children ask as they struggle with concepts of existence and nonexistence. In the second chapter, "Faraway Places," we look at the questions children ask to explore distant landscapes. In the third chapter, "Looking into the Future," we explore the kinds of questions children ask as they try recapture their past and predict their future. At the end of each chapter, we discuss ways in which parents can use their children's questions as the springboard to extended conversations.

Chapter 1
MATTERS OF LIFE AND DEATH

THE ANSWERS

"When did the world begin and how?"
I asked a lamb, a goat, a cow:

"What's it all about and why?"
I asked a hog as he went by:

"Where will the whole thing end, and when?"
I asked a duck, a goose, a hen:

And I copied all the answers too,
A quack, a honk, an oink, a moo.

—ROBERT CLAIRMONT

When Allison accompanied her mother to the obstetrician, the nurse let her listen to the baby's heartbeat. As soon as the nurse left the room, Allison questioned her mother, "Mommy, when I listen to the baby with that thing does she hear me back?"

Like Allison, preschool children are beginning to discover some of the properties of life. They know that being alive means hearing, feeling, seeing, talking, and being able to move. They are aware of life around them and are attracted to things that change. At least on an intuitive level, young children know the difference between animate and inanimate objects. A child who has just learned to walk will step on top of a stone and walk around a turtle.

Understanding the properties of life is not an easy task. Life means changes that are both gradual and sudden, short-term and long-term. Life means a beginning and an end. As adults we are accustomed to these changes. For preschool children, growth, birth, and death are new discoveries. As they investigate the properties of life, young children are confronted with its essential mystery.

Birth

Birth is not a secretive process in our society, and so children become aware of it quite early. Even if their own mothers are not pregnant with future sisters and brothers, children soon notice pregnant women. Pregnancy is announced with special clothes, sustained with exercise classes, and often culminates in a well-photographed finale. Parents generally feel comfortable answering their children's questions about pregnancy by telling them that a new baby is growing inside the mother. If children have the opportunity, they enjoy feeling the movement of the developing baby, and they may ask further questions about life inside the uterus: How does the baby eat? Is the baby sleepy now? Does the baby love me? When you take a drink of water does the baby get wet?

Preschool children are particularly curious about how the baby will get out. Judging the baby to be about the size of the mother's belly, it must seem like an impossible problem. Perhaps this was the question that led previous generations to concoct stories about storks delivering babies, but today's parents are generally not embarrassed. They tell the children that the baby is pushed out of the vagina, which stretches until the opening is big enough. Most children seem satisfied with this rather preposterous truth, although it is hard to know if they really accept it. Those children who take their parents seriously may have further questions:

Sherri: When I came out, did it hurt?

Mother: Well, just a little bit, but the doctor fixed it, and it was all right.

From this straightforward beginning, a preschool child's interest in birth can take several different twists. Some children become very interested in their own ability to make babies. The question becomes: How do babies get started? Despite their enlightened approach to sex, many parents hedge when answering this question. They talk vaguely about babies getting started when a man and woman give each other love. They take refuge in the metaphorical image of the father planting a seed in the mother. Some ascribe the feat to God, who makes all babies. A few parents forge ahead with a description of physical sex.

All of these explanations tend to have the same effect—they produce confusion:

Terry: How did Daddy give you love?

Mother: Well, he just gave me a little seed of love. I took the little seed of love, and it started growing into a baby in my stomach.

Terry: Did you eat me?

Chip: Does the daddy put the sperm in with his penis?

Mother: Yes.

Chip: Oh, it's in the wee-wee.

Although the most careful explanation may not clear up their confusion, preschool children can grasp some parameters about conception. They can understand that fathers never have babies because they don't have a uterus. They can become aware that only grown-ups start babies and that the process requires both a mother and a father. Finally, they can learn that mothers and fathers make a decision to start a baby. Children who grasp these fundamentals are not likely to become preoccupied with the possibility of being or becoming pregnant. Their curiosity about conception is temporarily satisfied.

A second line of questioning that children are likely to pursue concerns the way generations are linked. Jeff uncovered this connection by accident:

Jeff: You've got someone growing in your stomach, right, Nana?

Nana: No, not now.

Jeff: But you did have, right?

Nana: Yes, a long time ago, I had my babies a long time ago.

Jeff: What happened to them? They died, right?

Nana: No, they grew up.

Jeff: Where are they?

Nana: Well, your Mommy's right here, and Uncle Vincent is my other baby.

More often children gradually piece together the relationship between their parents and grandparents. They notice that Grandpa and Grandma are also called Mom and Dad. They hear stories and see pictures of their parents as children. Struggling to make sense out of this new information, the children often repeat what parents tell them. "My Grandma is your mother," Jamie intoned solemnly, as if asking her parents for confirmation.

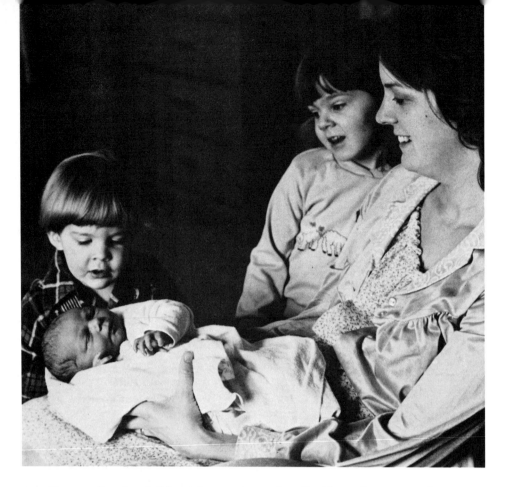

Eventually, the children demonstrate that the idea is becoming their own. "Are you talking about your mother or my mother?" Jamie teased when she overheard her parents discussing Grandma. Later she surprised Grandma by asking, "Where are your Mom and Dad?" Jeff, who at first did not know Nana was a mother, subsequently realized she also had been a baby:

Jeff: Nana wasn't always alive.

Mother: That's right. Nana was conceived in her mother's stomach, and she was born to her mother.

Jeff: Well, her mother wasn't always alive.

Mother: Yes, she was conceived. Her name was Mama Cecina, but she's dead now.

Continuing the conversation, Jeff showed there were limits to his new insight:

Jeff: Gorillas weren't never alive.

Mother: Yes, they were conceived also.

Jeff: Was King Kong conceived?

Mother: Yes, he was a baby gorilla once.

Jeff: No, he was always King Kong.

Preschool children inevitably reach a limit when they keep trying to extend the generational sequence back in time. Sherri asked her mother how the first person in the world had a baby. John asked who was born before anybody else. Kristin wondered who "made God alive." There are no easy answers to these questions. We can appreciate Kenneth's bewilderment when his older sister tried to explain evolution to him. Turning to his father he asked in disbelief, "Was Great-Grandmother ever a monkey?"

A third birth theme that preschool children try to understand concerns the period before their own conception. The subject may arise innocently when parents and children are talking about events in the past:

Brian: Where was I when you lived in Hawaii?

Mother: You weren't born yet.

Brian: But where was I?

Like Brian, most preschool children will not accept the idea of nonexistence once they become aware of this puzzle. Parents who respond by telling children they were with God have more success, for at least heaven is a specific place. Other children conclude, by themselves, that they previously lived in another family or that they always existed inside their mothers. "I was just very, very, very tiny," Amelia explained to her parents. Benjamin's mother, who was being driven to distraction by his questions, told Benjamin that he had been in her thoughts. This idea, which satisfied Benjamin, seems to meet the spirit, if not the letter, of the situation.

Although a young child's interest in birth most often takes the form of a conversation with parents, birth themes are also evident in imaginative play. Children whose mothers are pregnant are especially prone to act out the sequence of prenatal growth and delivery. When Jennifer's mother was pregnant, Jennifer lined up all her stuffed animals. Using a stethoscope to listen to their stomachs, she spoke to each animal in turn: "Camel, you have a baby camel in your tummy. . . . Pooh Bear, you have a baby Pooh. . . . Curious George, you have a baby George. . . ."

Death

Just as being alive means you were born it also means you will die. Parents are understandably reluctant to expose preschool children to death. However, children discover it anyway, even if no close relative dies during the preschool years. Death is all around us. Bugs are killed without a second thought and meat from dead animals is served at the family table. Pets, whose life expectancies are short, often die while children are still young. Above all else, death, both feigned and real, appears on television.

Preschool children ask questions about these different manifestations of death; but the focus of their concern is quite personal. When Emily's grandfather died, she asked her mother if grandma was going to die too. Jamie, after seeing a program about a single mother, assumed that her dad was going to die. "Mommy," she asked, "will I get a new dad when Daddy dies?" When Naomi's dog died, Naomi's first concern was about her own death. "Mommy, will you get another daughter when I die?"

In attempting to quiet their children's anxiety about death, parents often link death with old age. They admit that the children, and other family members, will die, but they stress that it will not happen for a long time. Many parents explain death as occurring because our bodies wear out.

On the surface, this approach relieves the children, and their questions usually stop for the time being. Beneath the surface, the children seem to remain troubled about death, for the issue periodically arises. One sign of continued concern is a child's attempts to find an exception to the universality of death. In the following conversation, it is not hard to see Joey's hope that perhaps, just perhaps, it is possible to escape death:

Joey: Will Joe the barber get dead?

Dad: Yes.

Joey: Will the church guy?

Dad: You mean the priest? Yes, he will die too.

Joey: The whole neighborhood's going to get dead?

Dad: Yes.

Joey: Even Mickey Mouse?

Questions about what happens after death are another sign that children are looking more closely into this subject. Initially, the children may be curious about funerals and how we dispose of dead bodies. The existence of cemetaries, where a seemingly endless number of dead people are buried, can come as quite a surprise. Thinking further about the idea of being buried, the children begin to realize the physical consequences of death:

Andy: Are you happy when you're dead?

Mother: No.

Andy: Are you sad?

Mother: No, you don't feel anything.

Andy: Do you move when you die?

Mother: No.

Andy: Can you play when you're dead?

Mother: No, you can't do anything.

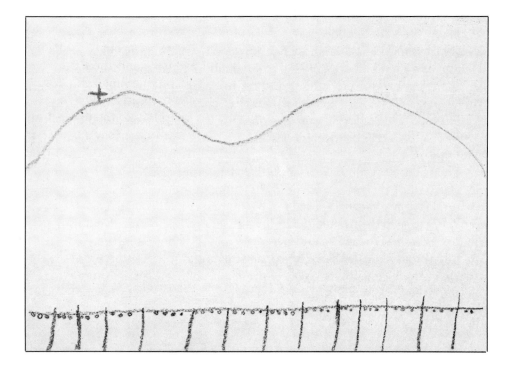

Parents who believe in an afterlife would answer Andy's questions somewhat differently, of course. However, even then children sense that physical existence as they have known it will cease. Whatever heaven may be like, it does not seem worth an immediate visit:

Terry: How do people get down from God?

Mother: Well, they don't want to come down. It's so beautiful up there. They love it.

Terry: I don't want to go up to heaven.

Mother: I don't want you to, either.

Terry: I don't want you to go up.

Mother: Well, I don't plan to go soon.

Children eventually recognize flaws or incomplete responses in their parents' explanations of death and want to pursue the topic further. They realize that death is not restricted to old age but can be caused by many dangerous situations. Car accidents, for example, are a life-threatening danger that parents talk a lot about while they drive. As comedian George Carlin noted, slower drivers who get in our way are "idiots," faster drivers who zip by us are "maniacs." Preschool children are attentive to such comments and often want to converse about car accidents they observe along the road.

Many preschool children are also very sensitive to the danger of being attacked by an animal. These dangerous creatures range from everyday acquaintances—bumblebees, spiders, and neighborhood dogs—to exotic animals, like lions, tigers, and crocodiles, and on to completely imaginary monsters, witches, and giants. In their questions, the children often try to clarify the whereabouts of a dangerous creature. Relatively familiar bees and spiders have a habit of appearing unexpectedly; who knows when a crocodile or giant might show up?

The children frequently assume that dangerous creatures like to eat people. Having just recently discovered that animals sometimes eat each other, it is natural for the children to exaggerate this pattern. Of course, fairy tales lend credibility to such theorizing. If witches and giants feast on small children, then the diet of lions, crocodiles, and even the dog next door might be similar.

Life-threatening dangers, like car accidents and animal attacks, are a recurrent theme in the imaginative play of preschool children. "Watch out," Michael told Jennie as they swung together. "There's alligators down there." The two friends liked to pretend that they were swinging over an alligator pit. "Ooh, I fell in," yelled Jennie, rolling on the ground. Lying still, she announced, "I'm dead." "I'll make you come alive," Michael assured her as he pointed his finger at her and made a high-pitched "laser" sound.

In imaginative play, sudden death is matched by sudden resurrection. This reversibility undoubtedly helps children cope with their discovery of death. At the same time, it alerts us to the fact that they are becoming aware of and anxious about the permanence of death.

Life is perilous in many ways, and preschool children can become worried about other dangers, such as illness, fire, or kidnapping. In each instance, they explore, through conversation and play, possible deviations from a "normal" death in old age. Usually the prospect of a premature death does not terrify them, but it is nevertheless a real and unresolved concern for a period of time.

Growth

Being alive means that between birth and death you will grow. Since the process of growth is imperceptible, preschool children are especially interested in body parts that grow or change rapidly. Hair is a prominent example of growth. On top of the head, it grows quickly enough to necessitate periodic trimming. On a man's chin, it needs to be shaved daily. Children often find it surprising that it does not hurt to cut hair. Although hair clearly grows, it also falls out. In fact, so much may fall out that a grown-up becomes bald. The body hair of parents is distributed in a dramatic pattern. They have hair under their arms, pubic hair, and perhaps hair on their chests. Preschool children notice these peculiarities of hair, and they wonder about its unpredictable growth. Will they have hairy legs someday? How long will their hair grow if it is not cut? Could a person grow as much body hair as a shaggy dog?

Skin is another part that grows almost fast enough to watch. New skin can be seen under a scab or blister. Cuts are sealed as if by magic. Just as the growth of hair changes with age, so does skin. The skin of teenagers and adults develops imperfections, like moles, freckles, and pimples. Very old people's skin grows in wrinkles and often has a mottled appearance. Again, preschool children notice these patterns. They marvel at the body's ability to build skin, and they wonder when their skin will change.

Changes in hair and skin are more often the subject of a conversation than an imaginary play theme, perhaps because suitable props are not readily available. Both girls and boys do enjoy pretending to shave or to put on makeup. In fact, the children now feel secure enough to alter their appearance radically. They revel in wearing masks and wigs. If allowed, they will draw elaborate designs on their skin with felt-tipped pens. The object of these dress-up routines, of course, is to appear older, bigger, or stronger.

Sometimes preschool children wonder if they really are growing bigger. Typically parents assure them that if they eat the right foods, they will grow. Although the children usually do not take to heart these lectures about nutrition, they do accept the idea that eating will lead to growth. Still, the end point of growth is unclear. Billy seemed to assume that he would grow into a giant:

Billy: When I get older, will I grow out of this house?

Mother: What do you mean? Will you get too tall for it?

Billy: Will I be tall and go through the ceiling?

Other children posit a reverse pattern, in which people first grow bigger and then grow smaller again. Children may think that the end point of growth is a matter of choice. Parents can explain that adults stop growing taller (although not heavier or stronger), but it is difficult for preschool children to see so far into the future. Frequently, their understanding of growth is based more on their wishes than on biological facts.

Suggestions for Parents

In discussing how preschool children explore what it means to be alive, we have focused on three broad concepts: birth, death, and growth. Many other ideas can be related to life and can be the object of a young child's curiosity. Preschool children are learning elementary information about respiration, circulation, the nervous system, and much more. They are developing a concept of germs and a theory about how medicine combats illness. All of these new ideas are interrelated, and by being open to conversations about life, parents give their children a chance to move from one topic to another.

When children become curious about birth, death, or growth, parents can enrich conversation by providing relevant experiences. Opportunities to touch and play with a newborn baby, photographs of family members as babies, and mementoes from a child's infancy will stimulate further conversations about birth. Reading a children's story about death or visiting a cemetery can help clarify a child's questions about death. Planting a garden or taking care of a baby animal highlights the process of growth.

The most difficult conversations occur when preschool children lose a close friend or relative through death. In their desire to comfort children, parents may talk about death as being like sleep. They may refer to the dead person as resting, or being at peace. Well meaning as these phrases are, they can further frighten young children, for they link death with relaxation and going to sleep. A better approach is to emphasize that a dead person does not hurt in any way.

The child's grief centers on the fact that death means separation. Parents can try to direct conversations toward pleasant memories, for this is a link we still have with those who have died. Remembering is facilitated by giving the child a photograph of the dead person, or something that belonged to him or her. Even the funeral can be remembered in a positive way: the fancy coffin, the bright flowers, the natural beauty of the cemetery.

At the same time, it is important to let young children express their grief. Parents can acknowledge children's feelings of sadness and anger while assuring them that they are in no way responsible for the loss of the loved one. Preschool children may find it particularly hard to accept the apparent senselessness of human death because they believe that important events serve some human purpose or have been caused by human intent.

One of the ways preschool children explore death is to include it in their pretend play. The same is true to a lesser extent of birth and growth. Parents can allow, even support, the children's efforts to create imaginary death scenes and funerals, or periods of imaginary pregnancy and delivery.

An enjoyable way to extend a child's conversation about the life process is to talk about the similarities and differences between people and animals. Many young children have a natural empathy for animals, and their respect for life is strengthened as they realize that animals, like people, are born, grow, and

die. Within this common pattern, however, are a wealth of interesting and amusing differences. Some animals are hatched rather than born. Some are born with their eyes closed. Some are born without a father in the family. Each animal grows to a characteristic size. Some are small enough to live in little holes; others, having no home, keep wandering from spot to spot. All animals die, but their life expectancies are radically different. Some live peaceably, eating grass to survive. Some hunt other animals and kill them for food.

There is no particular set of comparisons between animals and humans that preschool children ought to discuss. It simply is fun to explore our kinship with other animals, to play with our observations, and imagine a different sort of life. What would it be like to be hatched from an egg like a bird, to live in a nest until one day you started to fly? You could fly over fences, streets, rivers, go wherever you wanted. Of course, you'd have to sleep in a tree and eat worms. And you would have to make sure a cat didn't catch you and eat you for dinner.

In this chapter we have discussed some of the mysteries that preschool children discover as they talk about what it means to be alive. They learn that all people were once babies who grew inside their mothers. They have some understanding of how families are continued from one generation to the next and when it will be their turn to be parents. They know that everyone must die, and they are aware that death can be caused by many dangers. They know that they are growing, and they have learned about some of the ways their bodies will change with age.

Finding out what it means to be alive is a serious business with preschool children. The questions they ask parents are truly matters of life and death. As parents seek out appropriate answers to their children's persistent questioning, they find themselves walking a tightrope. On the one hand, they want to be truthful with their children and provide answers that are credible. On the other hand, they don't want their children to get anxious or confused. For every one of us, the time comes when we have to admit to our children that although we are perfectly willing to talk, we don't know all the answers.

Chapter 2
FARAWAY PLACES

Pussy cat, pussy cat,
Where have you been?
I've been to London
To visit the Queen.

Pussy cat, pussy cat,
What did you there?
I frightened a little mouse
Under her chair.

As soon as they can crawl, babies show a strong urge to explore new territory, to see what is under the bed or up the stairs. Toddlers, once they have learned to open the front door, may try to walk down the street. Preschool children continue this pattern. They range farther and farther from home base in their explorations. At the same time, children become aware of even more distant places by taking trips, listening to stories, and watching television. As they talk with their parents about these faraway places, children begin to piece together a larger world.

"Guess what, Daddy?" Nicholas told his father one evening at dinner. "Mama and me saw the Blue Bomber today. [The Blue Bomber was a beat-up jeep owned by Nicholas' uncle.] It was getting fixed at a gas station—on Potato Road."

"But Potato Road is where Uncle Rick lives," Nicholas' dad replied. "I don't think there are any gas stations there."

"Yes," Nicholas insisted, "first we came to Potato Road and then we saw the Blue Bomber getting fixed."

In the past, the Blue Bomber had always been sitting in a driveway at the end of Potato Road. If the Blue Bomber could move, Nicholas reasoned, then so could Potato Road. Nicholas' error is typical of preschool children. It takes a number of years to integrate different bits of spatial information into a reliable map. Nevertheless, preschool children pursue several themes that provide useful information about faraway places. One of these themes is air travel.

Airplanes and Faraway Places

"When I'm ten," Aaron told his parents very seriously, "I'm going to New York and see the Mets."

"Why wait until you're ten?" his mother wondered.

"Then I'll be old enough to fly on a plane," was the immediate reply.

For many preschool children faraway places seem first and foremost to be places that you get to by airplane. The children have been attentive to airplanes passing overhead since they were toddlers. Now they understand that these planes bring special guests for visits and then carry them back home. Parents, and perhaps children too, leave on planes for faraway business trips and vacations.

The strong association between air travel and faraway places may lead to the misconception that these places are somewhere up in the air. True, the planes come back down to land, but are they landing on the same surface from which they took off? Without a clear understanding of how points on the earth are interconnected, faraway places may seem like separate worlds:

Andy: Are there people in the sky?

Mother: I don't think so. Some people think there are people on other planets, but no one has found them.

Andy: Do people go to the planets?

Mother: They've been to the moon. The planets are too far away.

Andy: Is California another planet?

Mother: No, it's faraway but not as far as the planets.

Andy: Is Disneyland another planet?

Mother: No, it's in the same state; it's not that faraway.

Andy: Where is the North Pole?

Mother: Way up on top of the world. You have to get there in a plane.

Andy: Is it in the air?

Interest in air travel stimulates a more advanced understanding of faraway places. Whether or not young children have the opportunity to travel in a plane, they become familiar with photographic images of the earth as seen from the air. A highway or city looks much like a road map and the earth actually looks like a globe. Of course, preschool children do not fully comprehend what they are seeing in photographs and television shows. Nevertheless, we should not underestimate the significance of this visual experience. The preschool children of today are used to seeing the world from a perspective that would have dumbfounded adults only a few generations ago.

Faraway Places and the Unusual

Preschool children also associate faraway places with the exotic and unusual. A trip to the zoo, for example, may highlight the fact that many of the animals live faraway. Reindeer come from the North Pole, penguins from the South Pole. Kangaroos, elephants, and giraffes live across the ocean. Television shows may give children a glimpse of dramatically different weather, geography, and life-styles. Children in the middle of the country are fascinated by characteristics of an ocean environment: hurricanes, volcanoes, skin diving, surfing, and so on. Conversely, those who live near the ocean are intrigued with inland environments: cattle ranches, huge farms, mountains, snow, and skiing.

Because preschool children do not have a precise way to measure distance, their play may reflect anxiety that certain unusual animals or weather will

suddenly turn up. "Don't worry, George," Jad told his stuffed monkey. "There aren't any wolves around here. They live in the forest." Later Jad's mother saw him open a closet and call for Sharon. "Who's Sharon?" she asked. "That's my pet wolf. I'm going to take her for a walk around the block." Unsure how far away the forest was, Jad had relieved the tension by creating a harmless "house wolf."

The popular story *Where the Wild Things Are* presents an image of faraway places that may be similar to one many young children have. Somewhere, faraway, live an incredible assortment of realistic but grotesque animal monsters. They seem to have nothing better to do than gnash their teeth, make horrible growling noises, and wait for children to visit them. Those who are not brave enough to stare the ferocious animals in the face are unlikely to come back. Even as adults, we may have such images in the back of our minds, perhaps a faraway jungle where danger lurks at every step.

The most unusual faraway place is outer space. Children are initially drawn to this environment by the technical grandeur of rockets and space shuttles. Space travelers need special suits to provide air and water and to protect them against extreme heat and cold. On a space walk, explorers must be tethered on

a rope so they won't float away. As preschool children become aware of these bizarre characteristics of space travel, outer space becomes an exciting place to talk about:

Michael: Rockets took man to the moon, right?

Mother: Right.

Michael: Do rockets go to all the stars in the sky?

Mother: No, stars are like big balls of fire. You can't land on them. You can only land on a solid planet like the earth or the moon.

The remoteness and immensity of outer space makes it hard for preschool-ers to imagine. Some preschool children struggle to understand the basic prem-ise that space, tangible though it seems, is out of normal reach:

Billy: Why can't we touch the sky?

Mother: It's too high.

Billy: Even if we used a ladder?

On the other hand, a child may turn away from the limited reality of fire and rock in space and become absorbed in an outer-space fantasy:

Jeff: Can we go to Mars?

Father: Sure.

Jeff: Then we'll see the Martians and say, "Take us to your leader."

Father: Yeah.

Jeff: I have to tell you one more thing. They're very tricky, right, Daddy? You have to be very careful, there might be a trap door, right, Daddy? If you see a crack, you have to walk in the middle.

Father: Sounds like good advice.

Jeff: Then, if you see a tiger on Mars, you have to watch out.

Time and Faraway Places

A final way that preschool children discover faraway places is by asking where the sun goes at night. The sun, they may be told, is shining somewhere else. At first the children are willing to settle for a vague impression about the other side of the world. But as their knowledge of distant places expands, they refine this initial notion. A child from the Midwest learns that his relatives in California still have an hour of daylight when he goes to bed. A child whose grandparents take a trip to Greece is excited to find out that they are approximately one meal ahead of her. While she is eating breakfast, they are having lunch; then by lunchtime, they are sitting down to dinner.

At best, such ideas are understood in an oversimplified way. Preschool children do not realize that time is the same when two places share the same longitude, nor do they understand that the seasons become more extreme as latitude increases. They have little if any idea what causes the cycle of day and night or the changes in season. It is a big enough idea to think about daylight coming from faraway places to the east and leaving for faraway places to the west. Parents should not be surprised if the form for this thinking is more poetic than scientific:

Terry: The day kills the night.

Mother: What do you mean?

Terry: The sun comes out and the sun kills the night.

Suggestions for Parents

We have outlined several ways that preschool children approach the subject of faraway places. The first thing you as parents can do is to observe which paths your child is most interested in following. Is your child drawn to the fact that faraway places can be reached quickly and dramatically by airplane? Or does your child like to talk about where unusual animals, weather, or geography can be found? Is your child curious about the daily disappearance of the sun? Perhaps he or she is following a path we have not described, for there are many alternatives that lead to the same exciting discoveries.

Whatever path your child seems to prefer, you can enrich his or her adventures along the way. Look for picture books that provide new information. Suppose, for example, your child keeps asking questions about sharks. This preoccupation suggests that your child would welcome more information about ocean environments. Books with pictures of animals that live in the ocean might lead to longer conversations about this and other faraway places. A child who likes to wear makeup and create flamboyant outfits might be interested in a book that shows jewelry and styles of dress from faraway countries.

Even more powerful than photographs are films. Be alert for televised information that links unusual animals and environments with faraway places. Programs of all kinds, including news and sports shows from around the world, provide an immediacy that is difficult to attain in any other way. "Daddy," Jenny blurted out one day. "Do you know where panda bears come from?" "What?" her father mumbled, momentarily confused by the sudden change in their conversation. "From China," Jenny continued triumphantly. "I saw it on *Sesame Street.*"

By themselves these programs may not affect preschool children very much. Often the segments are too long and presented with narration the children can not follow. Information about faraway places may be so mixed with the story line that it does not clearly stand out. Parents can magnify the impact of television information by watching shows with their children and commenting on points of interest. They sometimes can offer simplified interpretations of complicated narration. Their role as instructor, however, is a limited one. "Lindsey likes to watch *Heart of the Dragon,*" (a program about China), her mother told us. "She doesn't understand the program, but she notices details that interest her, like the chopsticks, the way people bow to each other, the different sounding music."

Parents will find opportunities to build on new visual experiences, whether through photographs or films, by anchoring them to something more tangible and personal. If your child likes to look at pictures of planes, take him to the airport to see the multitude of planes that are constantly coming and going. Seeing a plane pass overhead a parent might say, "That plane is going south— I think it's going to Grandma's house in Texas—what do you think?" Like real explorers, it is intriguing for preschool children to imagine heading off in a direction and eventually finding the chosen destination. Try to find aerial photographs of your neighborhood or city. Buy miniature plane models for imaginary trips at home or build a child-size "airplane" with blankets and chairs.

For a child who is interested in the unusual qualities of faraway places, parents can provide experiences that build an awareness of cultural differences. An experience could be as exotic as a trip to an authentic Japanese house in a museum or as ordinary as hearing the story of the little Dutch boy who put his finger in the dike. A child might enjoy a record of Greek belly-dancing music or a doll from Hawaii. Sometimes puzzles can be bought that picture children from different countries. Books are available that tell how holidays are celebrated throughout the world.

Perhaps the most natural opportunity for conversing about faraway places is when packing for a trip. The packing process becomes a preview of what is to come and can easily lead to further discussions. Together you can chose

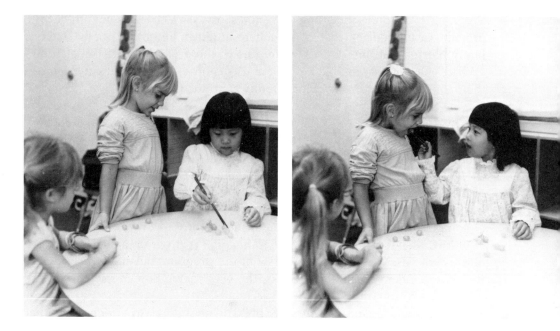

clothes according to the climate and activities of the faraway place. If no trip is planned, parents can help children pack for imaginary trips. Imaginary packing extends far beyond the clothes that will be needed. A child planning a mountain-climbing expedition will certainly need a snack for quick energy, binoculars for watching mountain sheep, and a shortwave radio for sending emergency messages.

By the end of the preschool period, most children realize that in some way places are represented on a map. Pointing to a particular shape on the map, the children proudly announce its name, much as they used to label pictures in a book. The relationships between the shapes are subject to gross miscalculation:

Michael: Which way is Miami?

Mother: That way.

Michael: Is Miami near Nevada?

Mother: Gosh, remember on the map? It's clear on the other side of the map.

Michael: Yeah, that's right.

Despite their confusion, children benefit from this rote learning. Being able to name some faraway places on a map sets the stage for later understanding of spatial relationships, just as rote counting stimulates children to begin counting objects. Particularly good is a map puzzle. Parents who like to make toys can make a homemade puzzle by putting a cardboard backing on a map of their own area. As the child puts the puzzle together, perhaps with the parents' help, it will give them a chance to talk about locations that have meaningful associations for the child.

In order to get beyond rote learning, parents can draw simple route maps. The map might show the way to a friend's house indicating right and left turns and several landmarks. Later on, a parent might draw a larger scale map consisting of major highways in a city, with nearby towns that are familiar to the child. Many parents find they can reduce a child's restlessness during a car trip by talking about landmarks that are coming up. Drawing route maps is an extension of this idea.

As children become interested in the spatial relationships between faraway places, parents can look for opportunities to introduce new information about distance and direction. Questons about the disappearance of the sun, for example, may lead to a talk about east and west. The term "north" might be introduced when discussing the location of Santa Claus. New information about distance can be expressed in terms that are within the understanding of the child. For a child who is just becoming aware of the magnitude of the number 100, parents might say, "Hawaii is more than a hundred miles away." For more advanced counters parents could say, "Many hundreds of miles," "More than a thousand miles," or "About three thousand miles."

When preschool children are particularly interested in faraway places, playing with a globe is appropriate. Having found where they live, the children enjoy locating the country that is on the opposite side of the globe. Vague notions about the other side of the world become more precise when linked with time. When it is noon here, it is midnight there. Just as we get up, they are getting ready for bed. Children who become fascinated with this game of global opposites will be interested in the relationship between hemispheres and seasons. Faraway places in the Southern Hemisphere (the bottom of the globe) have opposite seasons from those in the United States. Our Christmastime is like the Fourth of July weather for them. When the leaves come out on our trees, they are falling off of theirs.

Faraway places are a topic of fascination to preschool children. The impetus to explore this new frontier may be a trip or someone coming for a visit. In fact, faraway places are often identified with specific individuals: "California is where Uncle Joshua lives." Other times, faraway places are discovered by accident. The child sees something unusual, even frightening, asks questions, and discovers the existence of a faraway place.

Over a period of time, the children often identify particular characteristics of distant places that fascinate them. We have described some of these characteristics: accessible by airplane, unusual animals or vegetation, strange customs, a different time of day, unfamiliar weather. Children group these discoveries into rough categories: faraway places where it snows, where wild animals live, where astronauts go, and so forth. Some children seem to enjoy contrasting faraway places. For Jason, New York was contrasted with "the forest." Both were up north where it snowed. New York, a city of huge skyscrapers had no trees; the forest was thick with trees but had no buildings. People lived in New York. In fact, Jason's father flew to New York twice a week on business. The forest, on the other hand, was the home of wild animals, particularly those that frightened Jason: wolves, bears, and turtles.

Chapter 3
LOOKING INTO THE FUTURE

As Tommy Snooks and Bessy Brooks
Were walking out one Sunday,
Says Tommy Snooks and Bessy Brooks,
Tomorrow will be Monday.

Travis: Is today the day we go on the airplane?

Dad: No, ten more days.

Travis: I'm going on an airplane when I'm four,.right?

Dad: That's right, we're going to visit Grandpa in Minnesota and feed his cows.

Travis: And when I'm five, I'll ride a school bus to kindergarten.

Nearly every morning Travis and his father have a similar conversation. Travis is interested in talking about his plans for the future. The problem is that he is not sure when the future will arrive. The future, like faraway places or the life process, is a mystery to preschool children. By asking questions, however, children like Travis can gradually build a framework for measuring the future.

Time stretches out in both a forward and a backward direction. Children's awareness of how time expands, however, is not so symmetrical. A one- or two-year-old is much better at talking about the past than about the future. By the beginning of the preschool years, the child's notion of the past is filled with specific experiences that can be recounted in conversation. The future, on the other hand, is largely empty. Like Travis' airplane trip and school bus ride, a few signposts exist in an otherwise uncharted territory. By the end of the preschool years, as we will see in this chapter, the future has become an approachable topic of conversation. Being able to anticipate the future, the children can now enjoy it more fully.

Consolidating the Past

Preschool children may sound surprisingly sophisticated when referring to the recent past. At the dinner table one night, Jamie turned to her mother and remarked, "You haven't made that dish for a while." By the same token, children can recount the past to the point of tedium. "Mom, guess what?" Jackie began. "Today at school we had a parade, and I colored my hat with a red-and-blue crayon. I made the stripes going up this way. Then we put on our hats and we made a line outside the door. I held Alexis' hand. We went downstairs. . . ."

Whether they are being clever or tiresome, preschool children's ability to consolidate the past is impressive. When children begin to describe future events, it is understandable that they are most likely to talk about experiences that parallel those from the past. Karen, spotting some pumpkins on a roadside stand, remembered Halloween and wanted to talk about when it was coming back. Robin, after looking at photos of her last birthday party, began to plan her next one. Once children have organized the past, the future becomes much clearer.

"Nicholas, are you going to school Monday?" his grandmother asked.

"No, I can't," Nicholas explained, "cause we already had the last-day-of-school party."

Measuring the Future

Conversations about the future presuppose some system for measuring time. By three years of age, most children have a working knowledge of terms that refer to a vague but not distant future, terms like *next, later,* and *soon*. They may even be using these terms to ask about the family's daily plans. Three-year-olds also have some understanding of the word *tomorrow*. *Tomorrow*, however, is a floating term whose precise meaning is hard to capture because it keeps turning into today:

Brad: When is tomorrow?

Mother: When you wake up in the morning, that is tomorrow, but when it happens it will be today.

Brad: Is it ever going to be tomorrow?

As preschool children become more interested in the future, they need terms that are not as limited as *tomorrow* or as vague as *later* and *soon*. Parents start referring to days of the week, and gradually children become familiar with these special words. Some three-year-olds can actually recite all the names in order. More often preschool children focus on learning the names of days that are special to them. Hal, like many children, organized his week around a favorite television show. "Is *Knight Rider* on today?" he regularly asked his mother. "Not until Friday—that's three more days," she would respond. Other preschool children distinguish between the days they go to school and the days they don't. Michael referred to Monday, Wednesday, and Friday as "up" days, because he got up and went to school.

In the process of identifying special days of the week, the children gain a feeling for its length. Each time an episode of *Knight Rider* ends, Hal has to wait seven days before the show returns. This is a memorable lesson for a three- or four-year-old who assumes that television shows are at the beck and call of the viewer. Similarly, weekends, with their promise of a trip to the beach or lunch at McDonald's, are a week apart. Developing a crude notion of a week gives preschool children a useful unit of time. Phrases like *next week* or *in a week* signify that an event is several days away but not so far in the future as to be hopeless.

The week, as a unit of time, is tied to the near future. As adults, we rarely think in aggregates larger than six to eight weeks. For us, the month is the unit related to more distant events. For preschool children, however, the months have little meaning. As their attention focuses on units of time larger than a week, the future is organized around upcoming holidays and seasonal changes.

In fact, the four seasons seem to be blended with holidays to form a calendar of holiday seasons. Fall and Halloween combine to form a holiday season in which there is a grand mixture of pumpkins, witches, and colored leaves swirling down the block. Then comes the winter–Christmas season, followed by the spring–Easter season, and finally the summer–Fourth of July season. Sandwiched in between are minor seasons like Thanksgiving, Valentine's Day, and St. Patrick's Day. And in addition, of course, there are personal holidays in every family: birthdays, vacations, and other special occasions.

Preschool children vary in their holiday preferences, and parents differ in their manner of celebrating them. However, when the schools, stores, and television programs emphasize a holiday, it virtually guarantees that preschool children will be caught up in whatever event is approaching. Naturally, the children try to pinpoint the date. Not having a reliable system that extends beyond a week, their initial estimates may seem ludicrous:

Andy: When I wake up will it be Christmas?

Mother: No, it won't be Christmas for a couple of
          weeks.

Andy (Two months later):	Will next Tuesday be Valentine's, too?
Mother:	No, it won't. Valentine's comes only once a year.

With the help of such conversations, many preschool children progress to the point when they can accurately anticipate a holiday two or three weeks in advance.

The Years Ahead

The cycle of holidays is completed in one year, and many preschool children are interested in talking about this cycle. However, they usually remember only two or three holidays sequence. A more meaningful marker for a year is their birthday, when they clearly will be one year older. For a four-year-old, *next year* means *when I'm five.*

This personalized system for measuring years makes it difficult for the children to think about age differences. Brian wondered if he was still older than his cousin, Elizabeth. He had been four and she had been three; but now, since her birthday, they both were four. This kind of relationship is easier to sort out when children are a couple of years apart in age. "I'll always be older than Jessica," four-year-old Marcus exclaimed with satisfaction. He had figured out that his two-year-old sister might gain on him at times, but she would never catch up. If the children try to think about large differences in age, chances are they will get completely lost. Michael, for example, asked his mother, "Were you older than me when I was born?"

In thinking about the years ahead, preschool children have learned that growing older will also mean growing bigger. When they find that the correlation between age and size is not consistent, they are puzzled:

Michael (Referring to an old lady who was riding in the car): Is she a big lady?

Mother:　No, she is small.

Michael:　How can she be old and not big? Is Daddy bigger than Nana?

Mother:　Daddy's taller, but Nana's older.

Obviously, it is difficult for preschool children to project themselves years into the future. Imagining a job or career is a difficult task. The children do, however, become aware that adults earn money from their jobs, and they may want to discuss what they will buy as grown-ups. Alberto told his Daddy that when he got big and made lots of money he was going to buy "a robot, and a big, big box of crayons with points, and a new car that don't got a flat tire."

As we saw in Chapter 1, many children think of growing up as having a baby and being a parent. Having a baby is often associated with getting married, and this aspect of adulthood may trouble preschool children. They ask their parents whom they are going to marry. When their parents say they don't know, children try out some suggestions. They may suggest marrying siblings, friends of the same sex, or parents, only to find out that their parents won't sanction any of these choices. In effect, the children are left with the unappetizing probability that they will marry a stranger. In addition, the prospect of marriage implies separation from the only family they know. Children cannot imagine wanting to move away from their parents:

Kevin:　When I'm married, I'll still live in the same house with you, right?

Mother:　If you want to, you and your wife can live here. It will be nice for you to be married and have your own family.

Kevin:　But I don't want my own family. I just want you and Daddy.

The grade-school and high-school years are nearer and clearer to children. They may be interested in talking about the schools they will attend, or they ask questions about privileges they are looking forward to. A major theme in these conversations is increased physical freedom. Preschool children like to talk about being able to walk to school by themselves or ride their bikes in the neighborhood to visit friends and convenience stores on their own.

The pinnacle of physical freedom seems to reside in a driver's license. Not only do the children fantasize about the vehicles they will drive, they engage in considerable backseat driving. In fact, their questions and directives while riding in the car suggest that they envision being allowed to drive in the near future. They comment about stoplights and turn arrows, speed limits and one-way signs, lane markers and center lines:

Samantha: Are we going to go on the bumpy road?

Mother: You mean the road with speed bumps?

Samantha: Yeah.

Mother: No, we're not going that way.

Samantha: Well, don't go the way where the end died.

From all these conversations about the years ahead, preschool children begin to divide their own lifespan into rough age categories. They will be big children, teenagers, and then adults. Adulthood tends to be an undifferentiated period from the midtwenties to old age. Preschool children with teenage siblings or cousins will probably have a more complete view of the teenage period. Children who have frequent contact with elderly relatives or neighbors may have a separate category for old people. A limited number of key events will be associated with each of these age categories. None of them is likely to be elaborate, for preschool children are just learning to imagine the years ahead. Even one or two years into the future is a long time when compared with next week or the next holiday.

Suggestions for Parents

One of the curious characteristics of early memory is that children's most vivid memories tend to be negative rather than positive. As a three-year-old, Jennifer recalled a vacation to Hawaii when she was two years old. What she remembered was a string of misfortunes, from her viewpoint of course. Her doll's shoe got lost, the statue of a donkey near her room had a broken leg, and one morning her father couldn't get a newspaper at breakfast.

Although what is a calamity to a child may be trivial to an adult, children need opportunities to talk about past misfortunes. Bringing these memories into the light of conversation will reduce their intensity. Parents can also use these memories as a springboard to discuss the future. Jennifer's parents, for example, might ask her what she would do, now that she is four years old, if her doll's shoe got lost on vacation.

When encouraging preschool children to talk about the future, parents should start from an elementary point. Remember that the children are just beginning to use language in this way. A first step is to associate the idea of counting with the future. If children ask when a particular event will occur, parents can respond by telling them the number of days remaining. As their children show interest in learning the concept of a week, parents can emphasize that a week is seven days. A simple linear calendar might be made, indicating the seven days of the week and the special events that will occur that week.

More advanced calendars can be introduced as children show the ability to anticipate a period longer than a week. You can try a pad calendar. Write a single number on each page of the pad, starting with the number of days remaining until a holiday and then decreasing to zero (twenty days until Halloween, nineteen days, etc.). An alternative would be to lengthen the simple weekly calendar and label the squares with the days of the month, from the first to the holiday (February 1, 2 . . . 14—Valentine's Day). A third possibility, which is fun for children who can read numerals, is to make a special holiday calendar: Draw a large simple symbol for the holiday, such as an Easter egg for Easter, onto posterboard. On the Easter egg, cut out a U-shaped flap, as a window, for each day of the month before the holiday. Glue smaller pictures (simple drawings, like flowers, are fine) behind the windows so that the pictures can be seen when the windows are opened. Finally, write a date on each of the windows. As each day comes, the child can search for the date and open the window to see the picture.

Eventually, some preschool children show interest in the standard calendar. However, these calendars are too confusing for most preschool children because they include both a horizontal and vertical pattern. The calendars we have suggested are much simpler, and they are designed to highlight the special days that preschool children use to measure the future. Moreover, these homemade calendars allow at least a limited amount of handling. Children get to tear a page off the pad calendar, fold and unfold a linear calendar, or peek inside the windows of an holiday calendar.

Calendars help children anticipate the future, but other experiences give life to that anticipation. Preschool children love to be involved in decorating for a holiday. Naturally some decorations are too fragile or intricate for them to handle, but every holiday can include decorations that the children can put up or arrange.

Reading books with young children is an ideal preholiday activity, but don't limit yourself to books about the holiday. For Christmas or Chanukah, you can read books about winter, books about candles, or books about going shopping. Easter reading can be extended by reading books about bunnies, spring flowers, birds that lay eggs, or even a book about parades. Children who have a large collection of books might enjoy sorting some of them by holiday season. Then

the children can pick stories according to their mood. It will not be surprising if they think about Christmas during the middle of the summer or wish to read a story about a summer picnic during a winter storm.

Parents and children can "read" photo albums, looking at the pictures of past holidays and birthdays. Again, if a family has many pictures they can create separate albums for different holidays. An Easter album, for example, would show the family's celebration of that holiday, year by year. Parents and children can make holiday-season books using drawings and magazine pictures. The theme of a book might be "What we will do at Christmas," or "Things we like about winter."

As adults, we know that anticipation is translated into mental images of what we hope will happen. Preschool children like to act out their mental images by pretending. Part of a family's preparation for a holiday can be the creation of props for pretend celebrating. At Christmas, for example, children want to handle the presents long before it is time to open them. One possible solution is to wrap up some pretend presents, which can be opened and refilled as part of a child's play. There can be pretend Easter eggs (such as painted rocks) for mock hunts, dress-up clothes for experimenting with different Halloween costumes, pretend party favors for a birthday party, and so on.

Pretending is not limited to the period preceding a special occasion. Halloween costumes are good all year round, and the children may even want to pretend it's time for trick-or-treating. The same goes for pretending that it is Christmas Eve and Santa Claus is visiting. One way for parents to support these imaginary holiday seasons is to save old greeting cards and help their children decorate the house with them.

Of course, many conversational possibilities exist when parents and children explore what will happen during a holiday. Early in the holiday season, conversations center around preparations: the making of decorations for the house, the buying of presents, special baking and cooking projects. Later conversations focus on the sequence of events that will take place during the actual holiday:

Janet: Will the Easter Bunny come when I'm still sleeping?

Mother: That's what he did last year.

Janet: If I'm waked up, will he still come?

Mother: Easter Bunnies are very shy. If you think you hear his footsteps, close your eyes really tight.

Janet: And then can I go find the Easter eggs?

Mother: Yes, right after you eat your breakfast.

Then after the holiday, there are conversations about how the next holiday will be different. Having just learned about one holiday, preschool children often assume that the next holiday is going to be similar. After Halloween, Andy wondered what kind of costume he would wear for Christmas. Kristin expected the Christmas tree to be followed by an Easter tree. Finding out that the next holiday is altogether different makes the future even more exciting.

In this chapter we have been discussing ways that preschool children talk about the future. The children seem particularly dependent on parental support when it comes to these conversations. They learn much of their temporal vocabulary by listening to the speech of parents. More importantly, the children are drawn to the future when parents give them a chance to observe and participate in the plans. If there is little planning in a family or if the planning is done when the children are not around, they will have less incentive to talk about the future. Certainly it is fun to be given a surprise party, but on a regular basis, it is more satisfying to be involved in the preparation for special events.

As adults, we sometimes enter the land of wishes when thinking about the future. It is interesting, however, that the futuristic conversations between parents and preschool children tend to be on the realistic side. Children focus on the near future, and their aim is to identify what is really going to happen, what is really possible. Behind their attempts to talk about the future, there seems to be a message about autonomy: "Help me predict the future, so I can feel more in control."

Part II
DISCOVERY PLAY

Marcus was sitting in the bathtub playing with an empty shampoo bottle and a cube with holes on the bottom. When his mother suggested it was time to get out, Marc explained that he was too busy. As his mother watched, Marcus "sifted" cold water through the cube into the shampoo bottle. Next he turned on the hot water tap and "sifted" in some hot water. With his thumb covering the opening, he turned the shampoo bottle upside down and gave it a good shake. "I'm making a weather tester," he announced proudly.

In this section, our focus is on the child as discoverer. How does the child use active and manipulative play to answer questions and make discoveries about his world? In Chapter 4, "The Child As Athlete," we will look at ways in which children seek to discover the limits and capabilities of their own bodies. In Chapter 5, "The Child As Scientist," we will watch children explore the properties of living and nonliving things, discovering how some things fit together and come apart again. At the end of each chapter, we suggest ways in which parents can encourage discovery learning.

Chapter 4
THE CHILD AS ATHLETE

THE SWING

How do you like to go up in a swing,
Up in the air so blue?
Oh, I do think it the pleasantest thing
Ever a child can do!

Up in the air and over the wall,
Till I can see so wide,
Rivers and trees and cattle and all
Over the countryside—

Till I look down on the garden green,
Down on the roof so brown-
Up in the air I go flying again,
Up in the air and down!

—ROBERT LOUIS STEVENSON

"Watch me, watch me, I'm going to put my head all the way under.
. . . I'm doing a somersault. . . . I can touch the bottom. . . . Watch
me jump. . . . Watch me float on my back!"

As four-year-old Tami splashed around in the swimming pool, her demands for applause were nonstop. She had finally learned to put her head in the water and was close to learning to swim. Her mother, watching from the side, was called upon to admire each new accomplishment. When her mother tried to convince her to come out of the pool, Tami, despite chattering teeth, pleaded for five more minutes.

The accomplishment of a new physical skill is very important to preschool children. Perhaps they remember back to toddlerhood when each motor milestone was a cause for celebration. More likely, their delight with physical feats is associated with feelings of autonomy. The more things they can do with their bodies, the more independent they feel. Through play, they are discovering both the power and limitations of their own bodies.

In this chapter, we look at the two kinds of physical skills preschool children are working on and the kinds of motion they enjoy. There is certainly an overlap between these aspects of physical play, but there is also an important difference. When children focus on developing a motor skill, they are attempting to gain control of their bodies. When they explore sensations of motion, they focus on the thrill of abandoning control.

Preschool children possess many different physical skills that a parent or teacher can help develop. Although there is no single pattern that fits every child, we will focus on three clusters of skills that seem to be especially prominent in the exercise-play of preschool children: (1) climbing up and jumping down, (2) walking and running, and (3) gymnastic feats. These skills are ones the children practice over and over, and they delight in each new variation they discover.

Climbing Up and Jumping Down

Climbing up and jumping down form a natural routine. As we watch a toddler climbing on a stool and jumping down again, it is impossible to tell whether he or she is climbing for the joy of jumping or jumping for the joy of climbing. During the preschool years, children continue to practice and to elaborate their climbing and jumping skills. They master all the standard playground climbing structures and acquire an impressive repertoire of jumping skills.

One of the interesting elaborations of climbing and jumping is hanging from a bar and dropping to the ground. Climbing is easier than jumping, and children are likely to climb up to places that are too high to jump down from. At first they solve the problem by climbing partway down. Before long they discover a better solution. They hang by their arms from a top bar and drop to the ground. After a while, they find out that hanging has other possibilities. They can inch along as they hang or even swing their legs. Add inching and swinging together, and it is possible to move across a horizontal ladder. One preschool child described this feat as "walking with your hands through the air."

Our brief description of hanging stunts does not do justice to the individuality of the routines many preschool children develop. However, it does show just a few of the variations of the basic climbing-up–jumping-down activity. Indeed, climbing up and jumping down offers surprising opportunities for children to explore their coordination, strength and daring. Climbing up and jumping down can be a swimming pool routine that leads to diving. The challenge can be balance, as when preschool children climb up on a ledge, carefully walk its length, and then jump down.

The joyfulness that children exhibit as they face a new challenge or master a new feat is justification enough for encouraging jumping and climbing. At the same time, it is important to recognize how much children learn about themselves and their environment as they test and develop these skills.

Although children do not have the words to express what they are learning, climbing and jumping are an object lesson in gravity. When children climb a pole, they feel themselves resisting the downward pull of gravity. Jumping or sliding down gives them quite the opposite sensation. Gravity is working for them, and for one brief second, they have the delicious sensation of weightlessness. Years hence, when a teacher talks about gravity, they will have had the experience-base to understand the concept.

In addition to helping children learn about gravity, jumping and climbing feats help children acquire a working knowledge of spatial relationships. When a child makes the decision whether or not to jump from a ledge or hand-walk across a bar, he or she is making some pretty sophisticated calculations.

Walking and Running

The next cluster of skills, walking and running, is well developed by the age of three. Clearly, however, children learn to run with greater proficiency and control during the preschool years. Their gait becomes much smoother, and they learn to start, stop, and turn quickly without falling down.

More dramatic is the development of specialized forms of walking and running. One of the first to appear is hopping. When asked to jump over a low obstacle, two-year-olds tend to give a little hop. Three-year-olds learn to hop vigorously. For a while, in fact, they may hop continually, as if they were going to become rabbits. Human hopping is not worth much as a way of getting around, but it is immensely entertaining. As three-year-olds hop, they can hardly contain their giggling, and parents, caught up in the joke, find themselves hopping around, too. Sometime later, an even more peculiar behavior emerges: hopping on one foot. Again, the children go through a period of practice and experimentation, after which this unusual form of movement is channeled into games like hopscotch.

Hopping does live on in the form of the running broad jump. It takes several years of practice, however, to combine hopping and running skills. Standing at the edge of a puddle, the three-year-old is determined to jump over it. Then, at the last moment, concentration falters and the child stumbles right into the middle of the water. A year later, the child has a new idea. Now he or she will approach the puddle at a run, planning to sail across it with ease. Again, difficulty arises at a critical time, just when the child is choosing which foot to take off with. Undecided, the child sheepishly runs through the water on tiptoe.

This jumping-the-puddle business is beginning to look like a Three Stooges routine. More time and more mishaps follow. Finally, the confident five-year-old approaches the puddle and properly jumps off with his leading foot. For a split second, everything looks right, but then all too soon, the child lands with one foot partway across the puddle, like a ballet dancer in full stride. It will take still more time to learn that the longest jumps are accomplished by landing with two feet.

Another kind of specialized running/walking is even more silly and useless and therefore well suited to expressing exuberance and joy—skipping. Genuine skipping does not usually appear until children are near the end of the preschool period, or even past it. Its predecessor, galloping, is popular among three- to five-year-olds. Galloping presumably makes a person feel more like a horse; anyway, it's what a horse would do if it had only two legs.

There is right-footed and left-footed galloping, and skipping is alternating between the two, first leading with the right foot, then with the left. The feeling of freedom that comes from galloping and skipping is positively therapeutic. Children cannot help but feel lighthearted when they discover that their feet will work in this crazy way.

Like jumping and climbing, preschool children practice hopping and skipping just because they're fun to do, with no thought of additional benefits. Nevertheless, educators have long recognized a connection between mastering hopping and skipping and learning to read and write. The sense of balance, body awareness, left-right differentiation, and hand-eye coordination that children develop through hopping and skipping facilitate the acquisition of reading and writing skills.

Gymnastic Feats

A final cluster of skills that preschool children work on are gymnastic feats. Here, the generic activity is tumbling. Once they have mastered a somersault, children experiment with different body positions and contortions. They work on backward somersaults and cartwheels. They learn how to hold their bodies stiff to roll down a hill, or they engage in a twirling game until too dizzy to stand up. Having mastered the ability to stay erect, the children seem bent on discovering what the world would look like from another perspective.

Whether children are practicing running or gymnastic feats an important aspect of the activity is attracting the attention of other children. In the pre-

school years, sharing an exciting physical activity is a natural way to make friends. At four years old, Drew had developed a friendship with a mentally retarded peer. He described his friend to his mother: "Allen's brain doesn't work so good, but his arms and legs work fine."

Trying New Sports

Although preschool children spend much of their time practicing and extending old physical skills, they are fully aware that older children and grown-ups participate in a variety of different kinds of athletic activities. Grown-up sports often require special equipment and fancy uniforms and team cooperation. Naturally, preschool children are attracted to these activities.

When preschool children play at sports, their performance bears a strong resemblance to pretending. A game of tennis between two young preschoolers may be little more than randomly hitting a tennis ball, accompanied by phrases they've heard: "Net ball," "Your serve," "Love, one, two, seven." Older preschool children can temporarily organize teams. In the following example, most of the five-year-olds in a preschool class are involved in an impromptu basketball game. The result is impressive but not much like a real game of basketball.

After some initial confusion, the group splits into those who want to play and those who want to watch. With the exception of Shannon, everyone seems satisfied with his or her role. Karen, who has emerged as the leader of the game, explains to Shannon in a tone of insincere sweetness why she must watch instead of play, "I'm the coach. . . . I told you. . . . I just don't want you to play. . . . This is a hard game. . . . You can be in my baseball practice." Meanwhile Amanda has become the head cheerleader. She organizes three other watchers by telling them where to sit.

The game starts, coach Karen having determined that the teams will be Troy and Brian against Jason and Joey. There is no coordination between team members. Whoever has the ball runs in circles around a box (which serves as the basketball hoop), while the other three alternate between yelling for the ball and trying to block the path to the goal. Occasionally, someone gets close enough to the box to toss or drop in the ball. Karen, who is sitting inside an orange plastic tire, shouts out the score as she sees it and cheers on the ball carrier. The game stops several times because of disputes, and the boys go to Karen for arbitration. For example, Troy gets a rebound, which Jason considers unfair. Karen makes the two boys shake hands and warns Troy, "You better not do that again."

Some of the watchers begin to chant encouragement. Karen gathers them into a huddle and instructs them to cheer for Troy. Then she rushes back to the coach's circle in order to keep the boys playing. Sensing that fate is on his side, Troy yells several times, "We win." Apparently he has guessed right, for Karen signals the end of the game by leading away Jason, one of Troy's opponents. She puts her arm around him and says in her artificial adult voice, "You're a good loser." Then she finds Joey, Jason's supposed partner, and consoles him in the same way.

Experimenting with Force and Speed

The athletic feats of preschoolers, whether extensions of old skills or first efforts to play sports, give children the opportunity to learn about the capabilities of their bodies. They learn that people can climb, jump, and run in different ways. On a more subtle level, they learn to recognize and experiment with force and speed. These two ideas seem to be particularly intriguing to preschool children. They want to be as strong as possible and go as fast as they dare.

Force is involved in pushing a tire swing, kicking a ball, throwing a Frisbee, and many other physical activities. Sports equipment can dramatically magnify a child's sense of strength. The children love using equipment designed for hitting balls: golf clubs, bats, croquet mallets, tennis racquets, Ping-Pong paddles, and so on.

At an earlier age they could not coordinate a two-handed swing very effectively. But by age three to five, children are capable of stepping into a swing and putting real force behind it. Aiming the swing is trickier, and there often is a problem making contact with the ball. A ball on the ground is the surest target, and therefore children tend to use all of this equipment at ground level. Swinging at a rolling tennis ball, while hard on the racquet, is a thrilling demonstration of force for a preschool child.

Speed is also an important concept in most of these physical activities. In fact, children find that moderate increases in speed enhance most activities. Preschool children are not yet ready for the world of high speed, but they actively expand their limits. They try taller slides and learn how to gain speed by raising their legs. Or they may try out a variety of sliding techniques: sliding on their stomachs, sliding head first, even running down the slide. Such experiments seem to intensify the perception of speed. The trip down seems faster as it becomes more novel.

Now children race their bikes with greater abandon as they chase each other. Hills and steep driveways, which they once would have avoided, are seen as interesting challenges. Those who are practiced drivers of Big Wheels discover how to catapult their vehicles down several steps and still land right side up.

Whether we are watching preschool children swinging golf clubs with all their might or gritting their teeth in order to stay on a whirling merry-go-round, it is clear that more is involved in such activities than mere skill development. The children are experiencing powerful emotions. They have discovered the attractions of force and speed. "Watch me," shouted Angela, as she pumped her swing higher and higher. "I'm a bird, I'm an airplane, I'm Superwoman!"

Suggestions for Parents

Few preschool children are prepared for the complexities of participating in organized sports. However, all preschoolers can benefit from an introduction to the simpler skills in various athletic activities.

Of the team sports, the easiest one for preschool children to play is soccer. The children can practice dribbling the ball and kicking it into a homemade goal. A parent and child can play soccer by simply racing to the ball and kicking it in different directions around the yard. Basketball, if it involves a lightweight

ball and lowered standards, is also suitable for preschool children. They can dribble, shoot, and pass. The rules of baseball are considerably harder, and it is virtually impossible for preschool children to hit the ball within the limit of three strikes. If you use a tee to hold the ball—and if you're willing to explain the rules countless times—a version of baseball may emerge. Football, with preschool children, is strictly a pretend activity, a kind of tag in which one person carries a football.

For both baseball and football, parents can help their children develop throwing and catching skills, if the children are interested. Preschool children do not seem to play catch with each other very often, probably because it is too

discouraging to keep chasing the ball. Even with parents who throw the ball carefully and help retrieve errant balls, the children will want to go on to something else after ten or fifteen minutes. Playing catch with a balloon or a Frisbee, while not part of an "adult" sport, may prove to be more fun.

Parents can play a vital role in developing a child's talent for swimming. Because an important part of learning to swim is getting over the fear of water, parents are often better than professionals in giving children a good start. Opinions differ sharply as to the best way to teach children how to swim. Some parents are advocates of flotation devices that keep children feeling secure while they are learning the strokes. Other parents insist that children are not actually learning to swim until the flotation devices are removed. Whether or not a child uses a flotation device, here are some guidelines that you may want to consider:

- Start swimming lessons in an uncrowded pool or lake;

- Encourage your child to put her head under water but do not force the issue (practicing in the bathtub may be less frightening to your child);

- Let your child jump and play in the water before you begin your lesson;

- For the first lesson, pass your child back and forth between yourself and a partner;

- Move farther apart from your partner as your child is ready to move into the water alone;

- Do not work on strokes until your child can stay afloat dog-paddle style;

- Invite over as models children who swim just a little better than your child.

The playground is the most common arena for parents and preschool children to enjoy physical play. Parents are important participants and teachers. They must also be alert for dangerous situations. The following hazards are responsible for many of the accidents that occur on the playground:

- A merry-go-round that has a space between the turntable and the ground. Children can fall off and get an arm or foot caught underneath the spinning turntable;

- Swings, especially those with hard seats. Children can suffer head injuries when walking in front of or behind a moving swing;

- All climbing equipment that does not have a cushioned surface underneath, such as six inches of sand. There is no such thing as a climbing apparatus from which children can't fall;

- Horizontal bars, when an adult is not there to supervise. If a child tires halfway across, the only alternative is to drop down. Children can land on their elbows and receive serious injuries;

· Slides that do not have a landing with sides between the stairs and the slide. Children need a safe place to stand and wait their turn.

While it is important for parents to be aware of the kinds of equipment that can be dangerous, it is equally important not to be overprotective. Most preschool children have the capacity to judge for themselves how high they can climb and how far they can jump. When a piece of apparatus looks scary to them, they will make up excuses not to try it.

The physical skills preschool children develop play an important role in their relationships with other people. Parents take pride in the physical accomplishments of their children. The peer group admires physical prowess. In this chapter, however, we have described the development of physical skills as a means of self-discovery for preschool children. Physical play is an end in itself. During the preschool years, children discover that their bodies have surprising physical possibilities and they begin to appreciate the potential excitement of athletic force and speed.

All children tend to discover the same physical skills in the preschool years, although there are obvious differences in athletic interests and skill levels. Even more interesting are differences in personality. Some children are overly timid, while others seem too reckless. Some children are highly persistent, while others give up easily. Some children always have to win, while others would just as soon lose.

The differences in skill level and in personality that preschool children demonstrate as they try out physical feats are not necessarily significant. Some children who take a long time to develop their physical skills become star athletes. Overly cautious preschool children can become too daring in later years and vice versa. Our best advice to parents is to accept the future as an unknown and concentrate on finding physical activities that both you and your child enjoy.

Chapter 5
THE CHILD AS SCIENTIST

AT THE SEASIDE

When I was down beside the sea
A wooden spade they gave to me
To dig the sandy shore.

My holes were empty like a cup
In every hole the sea came up.
Till it could come no more.

—ROBERT LOUIS STEVENSON

As we watch Jerome playing in his backyard, we see signs of a budding scientist. At one moment, he is digging trenches in a mud pile behind his house, watching rivulets of water wind around his barricades. The next moment, he is filling his sand pail with mud and dumping it onto the driveway. After several pails of mud have been dumped, he hunts around for twigs that he plants on top of the pile. "That is a very good bear trap," he announces to no one in particular.

In this chapter, we investigate the scientific interests of the preschool child. We begin by describing his interest in physical things. What are the properties of matter and what kind of changes can he make? Next we look at the child's interest in the natural world. What interests him about plants and animals and what is he trying to find out? In the final section, "Suggestions for Parents," we look at ways of fostering the natural curiosity of children.

Investigating Physical Things

From an early age, children are attracted to semiliquid substances like mud and sand. At the same time, they are sometimes annoyed, or even frightened, when these substances stick to their skin. Despite this duality of emotions, preschool children are less tentative than toddlers about exploring different materials. They like to spread around a slimy substance or poke their fingers into gooey things.

In fact, sensory play seems to have a distinctly calming effect on preschool children. Sifting sand or pouring water is relaxing. The mood of the children mellows and they are ready for casual conversation:

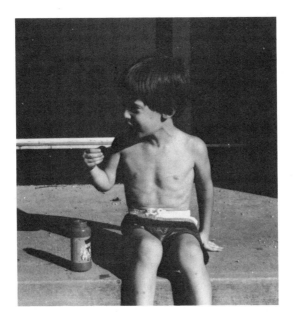

Kevin: I need the blue pail.

Katie: No, I'm using it. Here—take this.

Kevin: Hey, neat-oh. Look what I made!

Katie: Yeah—looks like an ice cream cone. I'll make vanilla.

Experiments

Sometimes sensory play is an occasion for systematic scientific investigation. The children go beyond the sensual pleasure of handling a substance and focus their attention on how the substance can be changed. More than that, the children concentrate on how a transformation can be reversed:

Zachary: Look at that. All the water from my bottle fit into the blue pail.

Laura: Yeah, that's neat. Try pouring it back again.

Zachary: Okay. Hold the bottle. Oops—don't let it spill.

As Zachary and Laura continue with their water play, they discover that they can keep changing containers and still have the same amount of water. This characteristic of water is obvious to adults, but for a preschool child, it is an important discovery.

While water play leads to spontaneous experiments with liquids and volume, sand play allows children to create solid forms with their hands. Given a pile of wet sand, children almost instinctively shape it into a castle or make a row of sand cakes. Although they may not describe their discoveries in words, children are learning that the shape of a substance can be changed without otherwise changing the substance.

Playing with clay or mud allows children to control transformations more easily. Mud can be compressed into a ball, then rolled out, then squeezed once more into a ball. Or perhaps it is transformed from a ball to a hot-dog shape and

then back again. A variation on this theme is to stamp a design into the mud or clay. The child can then "erase" the design by rubbing it with his finger or a roller.

Transformations can also be explored through solid objects that come apart and fit back together. As very parent knows, children learn how to take objects apart long before their third birthdays. Naturally they get better at it between the ages of three and five. The dramatic new development is an ability to use tools for this purpose.

A pair of scissors is unquestionably a favorite tool for taking things apart. At first when a child attempts to use scissors, the goal is simply to open and close the blades. Holding the scissors at right angles to the paper, which requires both skill and insight, can take time and help to accomplish. The next major break-through is learning how to continue the opening–closing motion until a paper is cut in half. The final step in cutting involves controlling the direction of the scissors. Once this is accomplished, the child is able to follow an outline with the scissors and cut out shapes without help.

Knives, like scissors, have a double value for children. Using a knife is both a grown-up skill and a means of taking things apart. Since knives are more dangerous than scissors, parents are rightfully concerned about their use. Interestingly enough, parents who do allow their children to use a knives report very few accidents. Children, for the most part, have a built in fear of danger, especially when that danger is in their own hands.

Jan's mother always involved her children in cooking. She had three sections in her cutlery drawer, one section for "little-girl" knives, one section for "big-girl" knives, and one section for "adult-only" knives. The highlight of turning four for Jan was graduating to the big-girl section of the drawer. "Now, I can use the knife with a 'stir-ated' edge," she told her daddy proudly.

Other tools for taking things apart are often too difficult for preschool children to operate successfully. A saw, for example, requires so much force that a child grows weary before the board is cut in two. A screwdriver slips when the child tries to remove screws but is useful for taking things apart by prying.

Preschool children who learn to take things apart will eventually want to fit the pieces together again. (In fact, a child using scissors may want to fit the paper together before he or she has fully taken it apart.) The ability of tools like glue, tape, and staples to combine pieces of paper is engrossing. Zachary, who had a particular love for saving odd bits and pieces of things, would spend a lot of time taping these pieces together. One day, he taped together a bracelet, some bits of string, several baseball cards, and a gum wrapper. "Look, Ma," he said proudly, holding up his creation. "I made a walkie-talkie."

The paper collages of preschool children are not usually fit together in any careful way. However, there are many objects that can fit together with a degree of precision. Between the ages of three and five, most children develop an interest in some set of objects with this potential. One child likes to dress and undress dolls, another builds with Legos, a third tries to make paper-clip chains. In different ways, each one of the children develops finer eye–hand coordination and becomes aware of spatial relationships on a miniature scale.

During the preschool period, children become noticeably better at fitting two objects together. They can see how the first object must be turned so that it will fit precisely with the second object, and they realize the angle with which force must be applied to join the two objects. However, they focus so intently on the process of fitting that they overlook the larger context. A child will work and work to get two puzzle pieces together, not noticing that they are different colors or that one is an edge piece and the other belongs in the middle of the puzzle.

In effect, a jigsaw puzzle looks like a simple "fit-together" kind of problem

when it really involves much more. In order to solve the problem efficiently, it is necessary to consider the relationship between the parts and the whole. Preschool children have difficulty thinking in this way, although there are signs they are making progress. With blocks or Legos younger children simply try to make as large a structure as possible. Later they are able to take into account part-whole relationships in order to construct particular forms. Similarly, younger preschool children focus on filling up every hole when playing with a pegboard, while older children fill up the board with intentional designs. This progress in creating structures or designs is generally slow, however. The ability to coordinate fitting together skills with larger plans remains limited and rigid. A child who has learned to make a Lego car or a Lite-Brite design tends to follow the same plan every time, according to a memorized formula.

The Naturalist

We have talked so far about ways in which children investigate their physical world, mixing and pouring, poking and pounding, pulling apart and sticking back together. In contrast to the child as a physical scientist, the child as a natural scientist is much more of an observer. He watches motionless as a spider spins a web or a bee sucks nectar from a flower. Eventually these observations lead to questions. What does the animal eat? Where does he live? Does he have sisters and brothers? As the child becomes more familiar with an animal, he searches for ways of making closer contact. He wants to bring the animal into his home where he can watch it more closely and take care of it.

The easiest way for children to make contact with an animal is by feeding it. Even very young children enjoy giving bread crumbs to the birds or feeding the ducks in the pond. Older children are ready to take on larger animals and may enjoy a trip to the zoo where they can feed monkeys and elephants. Paula was upset when one of the elephants ignored the peanut that she threw into its cage. "Daddy, that elephant don't like peanuts. Can I give him ice cream?"

Household pets provide children with an opportunity to make friends with an animal. The type of companionship a pet friend offers to a young child is determined for the most part by the kind of pet it is. Kittens are cuddly and playful but not very good as protectors. Rabbits are fun to feed and look at, but they may not want to be cuddled. Small dogs are good for chase games and ball play, but big dogs are better as protectors.

When we talked to parents of preschool children about their family pets, one point was made consistently. No matter how many pets there were in the house, the family dog had a special status. From the point of view of the preschool child, the dog was a family member. "You don't got to be scared of him," Jeffrey explained to a visitor who was looking timidly at their Great Dane. "He's a people dog."

Children who think about dogs as family members are likely to believe that dogs share human emotions. When Kenneth was visiting his cousins, he was introduced to their dachshund. Kenneth paid no attention to the dog until the family was on their way out for dinner. When he realized the dog was being left behind, his face registered shock. "But who is going to stay with Kim?" he asked plaintively. "Kim is only a baby."

While dogs and cats are the favorite pets of preschool children, close attachments to other kinds of animals are not unusual. Hans, who had a special fondness for insects and crawling things, developed a strong attachment to his pet snail, Snorpy. One day, his mother found Snorpy dead on the bottom of the

aquarium. She decided to save the shell for Hans as a way for him to remember his friend. With a look of horror, Hans took the shell from his mother and ran out of the room. A few minutes later, Hans came back to the room with quivering lips and teary eyes. "Mommy," he pleaded in a pathetic voice. "I just gave Snorpy a kiss because I miss him. Can we go to the lake and get another snail?"

Like Hans, many preschool children develop tender feelings for animals even when they do not have the status of family pets. Kenneth and his mother had visited a relative at the hospital and were waiting outside on the steps. While his mother was talking to a friend, Kenneth slipped from her side. A few seconds later, he returned carrying a dead blackbird. Caught by surprise, his mother told him to drop the bird immediately. "But, Mommy," Kenneth pleaded with tears in his eyes, "can't I take it to Emergency?"

Although most parents are pleased with their children's attachment to pets, the question of responsibility often comes up as a problem. Promises aside, preschool children are unreliable when it comes to the care of a pet. It would be easy, but probably inaccurate, to interpret this negligence as not caring. It is probably closer to the truth to say that children think of pets as belonging in the class of siblings. This puts the responsibility for their care clearly in the hands of the parents.

Although children as naturalists are especially interested in animals, they are also intrigued by things that grow, especially when they can be picked. Jamie found a dandelion in the backyard and couldn't make up her mind whether or not to pick it. Finally, she turned to her father, "Daddy, tell me, if I pick the flower off the plant is it still real?"

A preschool child's interest in flowers and plants goes beyond wanting to pick them. With an adult as a companion, preschool children often enjoy nature

walks. They can look for moss growing on the shady side of rocks, clusters of tiny wild flowers, weeds with an interesting smell, or leaves that are turning colors. Children also enjoy a nature hunt where they gather up nuts and seed pods.

As children pursue their interest in plants and animals, the questions they ask can be difficult to answer. They expect that parents will know the name of every weed or wild flower. They want to know why cats eat birds, why kittens don't have daddies, and why dogs have to die before they're as old as mommy. Many of the questions that are described in the first section of this book are inspired by the young child's feeling of kinship with other living things.

Suggestions for Parents

With very young children sensory play is associated with making a mess. The two-year-old pours the orange juice on the floor, finger paints with the chocolate pudding, and turns the bathroom into a disaster area with vigorous bathtub splashing. Although the preschool child is supposed to know better by now, the fun of mess making may outweigh internalized prohibitions. Once these prohibitions break down, preschool children are capable of making a truly grand mess.

Parents are rightfully disturbed by messiness when it occurs in the wrong place. Organizing sensory play outside, in the bathtub, or perhaps in the kitchen will enable the children to enjoy its benefits while not upsetting the order of the house.

The out-of-doors is the ideal place for messy play, proper clothing permitting. Mud and water are likely to be available, and even if the play gets exuberant, nothing can be damaged. In order to encourage scientific experimentation and add to the fun of mud play, supply your child with a variety of shovels, wooden spoons, and empty plastic containers of different shapes and sizes. If you are concerned about your child digging up the garden, fill a sandbox or tub with earth and let your child add water. Children often get interested in changing the consistency of the mud by adding different amounts of water.

Finger painting is another sensory activity that works well out-of-doors. To avoid torn and wasted paper, let your child finger paint on plastic or vinyl place mats or on an old plastic tablecloth. Make sure that there is a source of water around (a hose is ideal) that can wash away a finished picture. You may also want to give your child tools, such as cotton swabs, plastic knives, or jar lids that can be used to make designs on the finger painting.

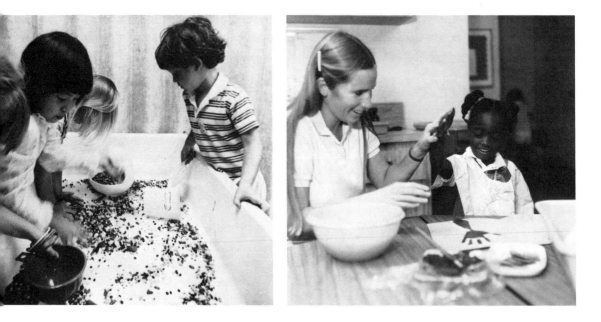

The bathtub is an ideal spot for sensory play with water, shaving cream, ice cubes, and soap bubbles. Again the play can be extended by simple props: plastic glasses and mugs, strainers, sifters, mixing spoons, funnels, and containers of different shapes and sizes. Inevitably, the play will turn to cooking and parents might be asked to taste a soapy ice cream soda. Interestingly enough, some parents object to this type of play because they think of it as regressive. Put this fear to rest. Sensory play not only leads to scientific discovery, it is also an end in itself. Because sensory play with liquid or semiliquid materials is relaxing and undemanding, it has a calming effect on children who tend to get overactive.

Moving from the bathroom to the kitchen provides opportunities for real as well as pretend cooking. With supervision, preschool children can learn to crack an egg, whip potatoes, mix Jell-O, and prepare their own sandwiches. These cooking activities do not always produce an edible product, but they do give children firsthand experience with creating transformations.

While sensory motor play with different kinds of semiliquids is fun and relaxing, putting together objects is an activity that offers a greater challenge and requires more concentration. One of the problems that children face is that the pieces of a fit-together toy are easy to lose or mix-up. You can help your child keep the pieces of a toy sorted by providing different colored boxes or containers for the different kinds of toys.

Decide on one or two types of put-together toys, and add to that collection rather than getting your child a set of each new toy that goes on the market. In selecting a put-together toy, take into account your child's limited muscle coordination. No matter how good your child is with constructing, toys that are too difficult to join together are bound to cause frustration.

The most satisfactory fit-together toys are ones that allow children to create a variety of products—toys like Bristle Blocks, Legos, Lite-Brite. Children can start with the initial challenge of fitting the pieces together and progress at their own rate toward planned construction. A trial-and-error strategy does not necessarily lead to frustration.

Puzzles, on the other hand, have a single solution. Some children seem to have a special talent for puzzles and can find the solution with no input from an adult. More frequently, children need help. One way to help a child is to do the puzzle yourself talking out loud about what you are doing. "Yes, this is the leg of a horse. It must go on the bottom of the puzzle. The horse is standing up. The horse's tail goes over here. Oops, it doesn't fit. Should I turn it the other way?"

A second solution is to help your child plan the puzzle by putting like pieces together. You could help your child make a pile of all the yellow pieces or all the pieces that are a part of a bunch of balloons. For more complicated jigsaw puzzles, you can help your child find the edges. If your child continues to have problems, you may want to do most of the puzzle yourself, letting him or her have the fun of putting in the last pieces.

Although preschool children are interested in construction toys and puzzles, they tend to leave these toys in a taken-apart state. Parents describe bins of Tinker Toy pieces, Lincoln Logs, and various sizes of Lego toys that are used occasionally for props in an imaginative play game but seldom for the purpose for which they were designed. Puzzles, too, if not rescued by a parent, are likely to meet the same fate. Even if the child has been successful in putting a puzzle together on several occasions, the end state of the puzzle is almost inevitably in pieces. Different colored containers, especially if they are strong and attractive, can help solve the construction-piece mix-ups. An effective way to keep puzzle pieces segregated is to color code them. For example, you can mark pieces of the fire-engine puzzle on the back side with a red X.

Caring for Plants and Animals

Although preschool children cannot be expected to take care of a plant or animal on a daily basis, they do love to participate in their care. Watering the plants, giving the dog a biscuit, or sprinkling the fish food into the aquarium are usually prized activities. As long as we are careful not to scold a child for an occasional slipup, preschool children will continue to think of their chores with pets as both a responsibility and a privilege.

Children's fascination with plants and animals extends to the out-of-doors. Preschool children have a special sensitivity to natural beauty especially on a small scale. They are intrigued with butterflies and bugs, lizards and snails, tiny flowers, rocks, acorns, or pine cones. Plan leisurely walks with your child so that

you can share these miniature discoveries. Encourage your child to collect rocks and shells by providing nonbreakable containers in which to save these treasures.

As children pursue their scientific interests, there are times when parents are delighted with their curiosity and other times when they are upset by all the mess. The more exuberant a child becomes as he digs in the mud, chases after

crawling things, or helps out in the kitchen, the more likely it is that parents will have to set limits. At the same time, parents need to think back to the questions that preschool children are asking about their world. As children actively observe, explore, and experiment with living and nonliving things, they are finding out some of the answers in ways they can understand.

In this chapter, we have looked at some of the ways in which preschool children carry out their scientific investigations. Although they may not be systematic and orderly, children are endowed with all the critical qualities of a true scientist—a passion for experimentation, a kinship with nature, an inborn sense of wonder, and an incessant need to know. Although from time to time we may be forced to admire a squirming earthworm or tolerate a messy kitchen, the scientific spirit that is ever present in young children must be preserved and nurtured.

Part III
CREATIVE PLAY

Christopher and his mother were driving to the mall:

Mother: What would you like to give your sister for her birthday?

Christopher: Three ice cream bars and three horns for her head that turn into boxes and long hair down to her feet.

Whether they are deadly serious or joking around, preschool children have the capacity to break away from the conventional and produce a creative and sometimes startling effect. Christopher's projected birthday gift for his sister combines his negative assessment of what she deserves with his recognition of what she wants.

In the two previous sections, "Conversational Play" and "Discovery Play," we looked at ways in which children take in and examine information about their environment. In this section, we will look at the ways that children restructure their discoveries, making new connections and creating novel products.

Section III is divided into three chapters. In Chapter 6, "Drawing and Building," we look at the ways children reconstruct their world by combining what they observe with what they imagine. In Chapter 7, "Playacting," we see children gathering props, trying out roles, and acting out play ideas. In Chapter 8, "Storytelling," we look at how children put their fantasies into story form. At the end of each chapter, we suggest ways for parents to support their children's creativity.

Chapter 6
DRAWING AND BUILDING

I had a little castle upon the sea sand
One half was water, the other was land;
I opened my little castle door, and guess what I found;
I found a fair lady with a cup in her hand;
The cup was golden, filled with wine;
Drink, fair lady, and thou shalt be mine.

Kevin, age four, was talking nonstop to himself as he scribbled busily on a sheet of paper:

Here comes the boat and all the peoples are in the boat. And a big hurricane comes—swish, swish, swish—and the waves are jumping and the sharks are jumping—whee—and the stars are falling out of the sky.

"The end," Kevin announced, proudly holding up his drawing, which by now was black with scribbles.

For children like Kevin, drawing, and even building, provides an opportunity to tell a story. However, for many preschool children, these forms of play do not produce elaborate narratives. The children simply enjoy creating an imaginary world with their pictures and block structures. Their goal is to design a set, not to produce a drama, and once they feel satisfied with their creations, they move on to a new activity.

As set designers, preschool children can acquire surprising skill. In this chapter we look first at the set designer as an artist, then at the set designer as a builder, and finally at ways parents can support the drawing and building of their preschoolers.

Scribbling

Drawing begins with scribbling for some children as early as one or two years of age. Scribbling continues to some extent throughout the preschool years although children are sometimes encouraged to give it up. "The school wants you to stay in the lines, but you and I know it's fun to scribble," Travis' dad assured him. As well as being fun, scribbling allows children to release angry

feelings that might otherwise provoke the disapproval of adults. An angry scribble is allowed; a wild exuberant scribble can even be beautiful.

Above and beyond the expressiveness of scribbling—the fun of it and the emotional release—preschool children use scribbling as a vehicle for imaginary play. If their drawing skills are not good enough to intentionally create representational figures, they can look for these figures in their completed scribbles. "I see a duck, I see a turtle," Erik shouted with excitement, pointing to a cluster of lines.

Such after-the-fact interpretations are arbitrary, but they do indicate that children are making the connection between drawing and pretending. Once this connection is in place, the children are primed to find images that have meaning for them. Erik had recently traveled from Florida to Colorado to visit his grandparents. Looking at a long red crayon scribble, he saw an imaginary trip:

> There once was a car that drove on the long highway to visit his grandmother. He stopped at lots of picnic grounds and rest areas, all different colors. He saw lots of grass. And finally he got to his grandmother's.

Scribbling is by definition an uninhibited style of drawing that lends itself to experimentation. Three-year-olds experiment with various forms: circles, ovals, zigzag lines, S-shaped lines, and parallel lines. The scribbles of older children may focus more on variations of shading and density. Throughout the preschool period, children experiment with colors in their scribbling. The result of all this practice is better control reflected in more precise drawing.

By the middle of the preschool period children usually are trying to draw recognizable figures. Parents who watch closely may actually see the initial transition from scribbling to representational drawing. The child creates a drawing in which several shapes or line elements are combined in a graphically coherent way. Often the drawing looks like a decorated circle. Perhaps there is a cross superimposed on a circle, a round sunlike design, or a circle with little irregular shapes floating inside. Such decorated circles are ideal for first drawings of people and animals. By the age of four many children also have learned to include rectangles in their drawings, and these rectangles are especially useful in drawing buildings and vehicles.

Representational Drawing

Once children start to draw representationally, it is fascinating for parents to observe their techniques. The first striking thing is the economy of elements children use. They create nearly all their images with combinations of circular and rectangular shapes, straight lines, and perhaps a few unique squiggles or shapes. Although the images children produce are not realistic, they are surprisingly successful in communicating their intent, and the end product is often playful and enchanting.

A second striking thing is that children draw each of their favorite figures as if they are following a formula. A person, a flower, or a car is constructed the same way each time. For the most part, these formulas are not imitations of another child's technique. Actually children at this age have difficulty copying another child's figure. Their new ideas evolve slowly as they practice and refine their own formulas.

Still another interesting characteristic of these first representational drawings is that the figures lack a common orientation. The daddy in the picture may be upside-down relative to his house, while clouds drift both above and below. This lack of a consistent ground line is indicative of the four-year-old artist's step-by-step technique. The child adds elements to the pictures as they come to mind, and orients each new figure according to the direction the paper is turned at the moment or according to where blank space can be found on the page.

In contrast to the spatial confusion between the various elements, each individual figure is generally coherent. By now the children are drawing human figures with arms and legs connected (although the arms might still be coming out of the head). The wheels of the bus are connected to the rest of the vehicle. Interestingly enough, these connecting elements almost never overlap. Long hair on a human figure flies out to the side to avoid touching the figure's body or arms. The four wheels of the car are all fully visible. Young artists seem to follow a rule: Every component in a drawing is entitled to its own space.

The drawing skills of a four-year-old limit the range of objects that can be drawn. However, most children find objects that represent their feelings and ideas. In choosing symbolic objects for their drawings, children seem to be influenced by other forms of pretending. Kenneth, who liked to sit on his throw rug and steer his ship through dangerous waters, drew a sailboat surrounded by sharks. Brenan, who was very interested in outer space, perfected his drawings of a martian.

Emergence of the Artist

By the end of the preschool period, many children have entered a stage of intensive drawing. Several factors seem to contribute to this burst of artwork. One factor is that the children are able to relinquish their rigid formulas for drawing. Although their repertoire of geometric shapes may not increase dramatically, children are able to combine these shapes in many different ways. Instead of having just one rigid pattern for drawing a human figure, they can vary the formula to produce different effects. In addition to his square-bodied martian characters, Brenan, at five, was able to draw a round-bodied daddy, an astronaut in a space suit, and a portrait of himself with very long arms and a chef's hat.

A second factor that contributes to the sophistication of late preschool drawing is the coordination of individual figures into a scene. Now, there is a consistent orientation throughout a drawing. In fact, the scenes of five-year-olds often demonstrate a pleasing balance and symmetry. This balance is accentuated by the fact that each figure still occupies a separate space, creating a flat but bold effect.

The bold quality of a five-year-old's drawing is further enhanced by an unrestrained use of bright colors. The children may outline a figure in one color and then fill it in solidly with a different color. These powerful, bright colors, combined with the flatness and symmetry, are reminiscent of dream images. Perhaps the drawings of five-year-olds are related, on an unconscious level, to their dreams.

A final factor, which is just emerging at the end of the preschool period, is the appearance of a continuous outline for a figure. Because this technique is difficult, new and unpredictable images can be created. A human figure may look more like a ghost. It may be endowed with very long arms and legs or gigantic hands and feet. At the same time, the continuous outline may allow the child to draw a wider range of animals and vehicles.

Although some preschool children try to depict action in their pictures, the strength of a young child's drawing lies in its power to evoke feelings. More than ever before, we see the energy of the five-year-old artist going into the depiction of mood and emotion. On his way home from the circus, Carlos drew a carnival scene that had a feeling of festive excitement. Celia, following her first experience with the death of a relative, drew a desolate landscape with a single cross in the distance. Patricia, who was a happy, carefree child, drew a field of flowers with a bright yellow sun in the corner. Whether the emotions they depict are happy, sad, or angry, the drawings of five-year-olds have an underlying air of confidence. For the moment at least, the children are satisfied with their productions and comfortable with their ability as artists.

Building

Building might be thought of as drawing in three dimensions. In this sense, it is more complex. In another way, building seems simpler because it is very concrete. A toddler who lines up his toy animals on the side of the bathtub is already involved in building. Indeed, building is a part of so many types of play that it is hard to isolate as a single activity. We tend to associate building with blocks, but play with other such media as sand and clay can also lead to building. When children use sheets and blankets to create structures, they are building. When they arrange objects inside the tent, they are building in a different way. Even children who create fancy dress-up outfits seem to be building as they try on different combinations of skirts, scarfs, jewelry, and hats.

In this chapter, we focus on block play because it is the clearest example of building. Keep in mind, however, that building skills are developed with many different kinds of material including the various types of fit-together building sets.

If there is a "scribbling stage" in block building, it does not seem particularly significant. Long before the preschool years, children name their block constructions and consider them representational. Like early drawings, these block creations are crude abstractions of real structures. A stack of blocks, with its tower effect, may represent an office building or a church. An irregular enclosure can serve as the outline for a house, a restaurant, or a pigpen. By the end of the preschool period, on the other hand, children who are interested in block building have learned to create structures that are detailed and elaborate. Three stages emerge in this evolution.

The first theme that avid builders discover is the power of repetition. A flat line of blocks can be reproduced again and again until the line has become a rectangular platform or floor. In the same way, a single tower of blocks can generate a cluster of towers that look like skyscrapers or a castle. We call this technique the *solid look*. Preschool children may start with rectangular floors and then add layers to form solid cubes. Or they may go from a cluster of irregular towers to regular patterns that look like staircases and pyramids.

The second technique, which contrasts with the solid look, involves the creation of internal space. This *hollow look* can emerge when children try

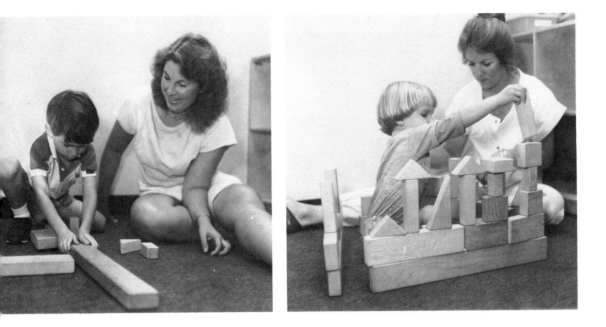

removing the inside of a solid form. Another early version of the hollow look is the arch, a crossbar resting on two supporting columns. Once preschool children discover how to create internal space, further insights follow. One is that the hollow look can be reproduced. Four- and five-year-old builders delight in constructing a series of connected pens or hollow rectangles. Similarly, they like to build a series of arches, one on top of the other. This multiplication of internal space, in various sizes and shapes, can create an intricate, even a spectacular, visual effect. Another insight is that internal space can be embellished with objects. Younger preschool children fill their pens with animals and cars; they stand miniature figures inside of arches. By the end of the preschool period, some children have learned to build furniture and other accessories for internal space.

The final development in preschool block building is the gradual awareness of three dimensions. Although blocks are three dimensional, children often use them in the beginning as one-dimensional points. They stack up blocks to make a line. Subsequently, they spend time exploring two-dimensional block structures. A series of pens, or a tower of arches, functions essentially as a two-dimensional figure. Toward the end of the preschool years, the children begin to realize the three-dimensional character of block building. When they make an enclosure, they want to build up the walls and add a roof. The arch structure becomes a genuine tunnel in which the children plan all three dimensions: the height, width, and length of the tunnel.

These three-dimensional structures combine the characteristics of both the solid and hollow look. The structures are stable and strong looking, but inside there is empty space. Preschool children are intrigued with their ability to create these secret spaces. They soon discover, however, that this space is not very practical if it is inaccessible. Therefore, as the children experiment with larger and more elaborate three-dimensional structures, they look for ways to create access to internal space. They may, as preschoolers, learn how to create caves and cubbyholes, how to add doors and windows, but the problem is a recurring one. The challenge for the budding architect is to create a three-dimensional structure that looks realistic but still allows hands to get inside and rearrange the interior.

Suggestions for Parents

In both drawing and building, a logical beginning point is to consider what materials your child will need. Because each child's interests are somewhat different, it is a good idea to experiment with many materials before investing heavily in any one direction. Look for opportunities to try different kinds, sizes, and colors of paper, different types of markers, crayons, and chalk. Is your child attracted to blackboards, laminated drawing boards, or Magic Slates? What about watercolors versus tempera paint? For building, try colored blocks as well as natural ones, small unit blocks, geometric-shape blocks, extralong or big blocks, and fit-together types like Legos. If you want to create homemade blocks, such as oversize Lincoln Logs made from 2×2s, experiment with a small set.

Having provided stimulating materials, parents then may wonder if participating in their child's play will help or hinder the development of creativity. Here we see a fairly sharp difference in practice between drawing and building. Parents rarely hesitate to help a child get started with a new set of blocks, while they hesitate to participate in drawing activities. Some parents are concerned about repressing their children's creativity. Others are worried about their own lack of talent. Although parents, for different reasons, may be hesitant to draw with their children, children are just as pleased to have their parents join them in drawing as they are when they join them in building. They are neither inhibited by a parent who draws very well nor critical of a parent who is completely devoid of talent.

Whether drawing or building, parents can watch for signs that their participation is overwhelming a preschool child. A child may continually insist that the parent do the drawing or building, indicating an "I can't" attitude. Or a child may adopt a perfectionist attitude and become overly angry and frustrated by his own mistakes. These signs do not necessarily mean that parents have been domineering in joint play. Some children are temperamentally predisposed toward such attitudes and develop them quickly when parents play with them.

The best response is to try substituting peer interaction. As children get more opportunities to draw and build with peers, they see that they are not helpless nor do they need to be perfect.

Parents also can try to develop a different way of participating in drawing and building. One idea is to say that you do not want to play right now but that when the drawing or block structure is finished you will tell a story about it. This approach shifts the responsibility for drawing and building to your child while still offering the stimulation of a parent's creativity. Before telling the story, ask if there is anything else your child wants to add to the picture, any other accessories or miniature props to be included in the block structure. Then, using the imaginary setting created by your child, weave the elements into a story that is simple enough to inspire future drawing and building.

Jason was working on an elaborate block structure that looked like a Disneyworld castle. When he succeeded in balancing the last of the blocks on the top of the structure, he ran to get his mother. Recognizing that Jason needed some help in deciding what to do next, his mother began a story.

"Look at that, Cinderella's castle is ready for occupancy! She will be so pleased. Do you know what happened to poor Cinderella last night?" As Jason's

mother continued the story, he listened with rapt attention. His grandiose block structure was even more important than he realized!

Parents who provide their children with a variety of building and drawing materials to foster artistic creativity may worry about the effect of coloring books. Certainly preschool children are not developing their own symbols or expressing their own feelings when they color printed pictures. However, if they are allowed to proceed as they please, these printed pictures often stimulate intensive color experimentation. Each part of a figure may be colored a different shade, so that a panda bear has pink legs, blue ears, a green face, and a purple body. A figure may be colored with rainbow stripes or some other design. Even after children have reached the point where they limit themselves to traditional colors, coloring books still encourage thought about color combinations.

Children who are interested in block building go through a similar phase when they try to copy the structures they see on the side of the box or in the instructions. Again, the children lose track, at least for a while, of their own imaginary ideas. If left alone, however, they usually settle for an imperfect copy of the illustrated construction, and in the process, they have experimented with some new forms.

The relationship between creativity and copying is not simple. Preschool children stamp their drawings and block constructions with their own personalities. At the same time, these artistic achievements reflect the visual experience of the children. No one can know ahead of time what new sights will later be copied in drawing and building. Parents can go far beyond coloring books and block illustrations in providing new ideas. Looking at the illustrations in children's books, at art books, or even at comic strips may trigger a new direction in drawing. New building ideas may come from books that show the skyline of a city or an aerial view of a housing development. Other pictures that could inspire ideas are photos of parks, playgrounds, and plazas, or drawings of medieval castles and forts. With each new visual experience, whether or not it becomes part of drawing and building, parents are helping children to a higher level of aesthetic sensitivity.

When preschool children draw and build they are learning about spatial relations, how to arrange and combine elements so that the whole is recognizable and pleasing to look at. The children also are learning how to express their feelings and ideas through pictures and block structures. They are developing their imagination. These two themes go hand in hand. Children's growing

ability to create representational symbols is associated with a growing ability to select emotionally vivid images.

Of course, drawing and building involve different media, and many preschool children have a preference for one or the other. However, and when preschool children participate in both activities the parallels between them are evident. Drawing and building are part of a larger domain, the creation of imaginary settings. In a literal sense this is the kind of creativity in which an image is constructed. The broad changes that take place in drawing and building can be seen whenever preschool children try to create a setting for pretend play. Rigidity gives way to flexibility, and haphazard construction is replaced by planning. As the children enter elementary school, their image-making ability matures, and they seem to be riding on a wave of artistic creativity.

Chapter 7
PLAY ACTING

PIRATE STORY

Three of us afloat in the meadow by the swing,
Three of us aboard in the basket on the lea.
Winds are in the air, they are blowing in the spring;
And waves are on the meadow like the waves there are at sea.

Where shall we adventure, to-day that we're afloat,
Wary of the weather and steering by a star?
Shall it be to Africa, a-steering of the boat,
To Providence, or Babylon, or off to Malabar?

Hi! but here's a squadron a-rowing on the sea—
Cattle on the meadow a-charging with a roar!
Quick, and we'll escape them, they're as mad as they can be,
The wicket is the harbor and the garden is the shore.

—ROBERT LOUIS STEVENSON

When they are drawing and building, the creativity of preschool children is directed toward the construction of an imaginary setting. In this chapter, we will look at another form of imaginary play, where the focus is on action, or more properly "acting." Acting out an imaginary role is a major way for preschool children to pretend. Once the stage has been set by gathering props or putting on costumes, the production begins:

Mandy: I'll be the mommy and you be the little girl. We go on a picnic. Now you sit down.

Mother: Is this where we're having the picnic?

Mandy: Yes, watch out for bugs. You want some milk?

Mother: Oh, I'd love some. This milk is delicious. What else are we going to eat?

Mandy: You see any bugs? Don't let the bugs bite you.

Mother: I'd like some dessert.

Mandy: I got some birthday cake. I cut you some?

Mother: Sounds good, but how about a cup of cocoa?

Mandy: Soon you get cocoa, I'm colding it. Let's sing Happy Birthday.

The challenge in playacting is to develop a script to keep the action going.
Mandy, a talkative three-year-old, moves the play forward by conversing with
her mother. During the preschool years, there is a dramatic increase in children's ability to elaborate roles and sequence events through language. Language enables the children to assign roles, resolve disputes, and suggest new
directions in the pretending. It is an interactive process in which one comment
leads to another and new ideas emerge to everyone's surprise.

Listening to the brief conversation between Mandy and her mother, we
can see three themes that stand out in the playacting of preschool children.
First, there is the theme of "belonging to a family." Mandy is playing with her
place in the family by reversing roles with her mother. Second, there is the
theme of fulfilling wishes. Mandy's picnic turns out to be a birthday party and
the main course a cake. The third theme is "feeling powerful" and often involves facing danger or overcoming something fearful. In the picnic scene,
danger never materializes because the bugs do not arrive. If they had, however,
we can be sure Mandy would have dispatched them triumphantly. We can learn
a great deal about the world of the preschooler by looking closely at each of
these themes in their playacting.

Family Play

Like Mandy, preschool children often reverse roles with their parents in pretend play. Parents enjoy acting like demanding children as much as children
enjoy being bossy parents. Still, parents may wonder at times, "Do I really
sound that nasty?" Probably not, at least most of the time, for preschoolers tend
to exaggerate their authority as pretend parents. Part of what is going on is the
natural capacity to enjoy acting angry or petulant. Whether parent or child, it
is fun to release mild hostility without suffering any real consequences. Addi-
tionally, young children may act overbearing to compensate for their lack of
real power in the family. Being the powerful center of an imaginary family
makes it easier to accept a place that is without much power in the real family.

For some preschool children, the family issue of greatest concern is not
differences in power between parents and children, but the difference in the
way parents relate to children and babies. "I want my bottle," four-year-old

Benjamin told his dad as he sat on his father's lap. "Gosh, did I forget your feeding time?" his father asked. "Here's your bottle." Benjamin reached out to accept the imaginary bottle and then pretended to drink it by noisily gurgling and smacking his lips. "Time to burp you," his father soon said. Not to be outdone by Benjamin's caricature of eating, he held Benjamin horizontally away from his body and then flung him upright over his shoulder. "Burp, baby" was the command, and after several more violent jiggles on dad's part and hiccupy giggles on Benjamin's part, the baby was put down "to crawl around for a while."

Reverting to a baby role may bother parents because it seems regressive. But in most cases, simply expressing the desire to be a baby helps children go on to accept their more grownup position in the family. Benjamin's dad facilitated this development by making the pretend play lighthearted. Turning the feeding ritual into a joke, but still one with lots of physical intimacy, brought the play to a natural ending point and highlighted the difference between real and pretend. Reducing the intensity of a pretend theme through humor is much more effective than trying to suppress the pretending altogether. As Benjamin's dad admitted, there are, of course, times when he doesn't feel very playful; he then tries to direct Benjamin's attention elsewhere.

A special family role that combines the power of a parent with the attention of a baby is the role of entertainer. This role might be called "the special child." Instead of growing older and more powerful, or younger and more dependent, the child stays the same age but puts on a special performance. The performance may be simple: Jenny hopped around the house and turned into a bunny. It may be noisy: Jason threw himself on the floor and turned into a vacuum cleaner that sucked up imaginary garbage. The child's goal is to show off his or her talent and gain the admiration of the audience.

Kevin's favorite activity was staging shows for his family. Preparations for his performances included putting together outlandish costumes, posting the next performance on the marquee outside his room, and setting up a row of chairs for his audience. With the versatility of a true showman, Kevin was costume designer, stage director, and playwright. He also acted out every part.

"Tonight you will see the great Captain Blue Star, and Raincoat Man, and T-Man and T-Man's brother, and T-Man's other brother and T-Man's other older brother, and Secret Agent Magnet Man, and White Mane Willy."

As children grow older, their interest shifts from playacting at home with the family to playacting with the peer group. As would be expected, peer group play is likely to be organized around family themes. As we listen to Lisa taking the part of mother on the school playground, the issue of dominance comes through loud and clear.

"Do up your seat belt," Lisa told Katie in a loud, strident voice. "We are not playing policeman—I am your mother. Now do up your seat belt like I said." Katie, who was pretending to be the baby in the family, grabbed Lisa's sunglasses. "You give them back, baby," Lisa demanded. "Some babies don't give them back," Katie replied stubbornly, but she did return them. Next Katie started to chew on her necklace. "Take that out of your mouth," Lisa warned. Arriving at a restaurant, Lisa and the other children ordered corned beef. "I want chicken," Katie said, being contrary to the end.

A pretend family of preschoolers often has a black sheep like Katie, a mischievous or disobedient child who serves as a foil for mom and the good brothers and sisters. By agreeing to disagree, the family has a reliable way to generate new plots.

Despite the changing role of fathers in America, preschool boys are less likely than girls to engage in family play. They do, however, re-create another family relationship regularly: that of man and dog. Man and dog seems to be akin to mother and child. The dominant boy can take care of his dog by feeding, brushing, and petting it, while the dog can reciprocate by being mischievous and protecting his master from strangers. Andrew demonstrated a clever way to recruit a large family of dogs. Seeing a boy playing nearby, he sent his favorite dog to attack the boy and ask him if he wanted to be a dog too. Each new member of the family then came into the playhouse and was affectionately patted by Andrew, before being sent abroad to bite and recruit another boy. Soon Andrew and the dogs were playing tag in the house, running around and around the kitchen table. For the winner, the prize was "a big bone" (a block of wood) from the refrigerator.

Comparing Mandy and her mother's picnic with the play among five-year-olds, it is obvious that the interaction has become wilder and less predictable. Even more impressive is the fact that the peer group is able to coordinate several different roles without adult assistance. The children have progressed to the point where they can agree on reciprocal roles (for example, those of mother and daughter), decide on how the two roles relate to each other, and work to maintain the relationship.

Wishes Can Come True

Sitting on his tricycle, Chad roars up to the television. In the process, his favorite stuffed friend, Kermit the Frog, falls off the back of the "motorcycle" and onto the floor. Quickly Chad retrieves Kermit and props him on the trike. With one hand on his hip and the other braced against the television set, Chad adopts a nonchalant posture and stares at his reflection in the darkened screen. "I'll take two hamburgers, four french fries, and six Cokes," he decisively informs his own image. Then, pretending the face in the screen has responded, he accepts an invisible bag of food, mounts his motorcycle once more, and departs with a flourish.

Chad's mother, who has seen this scene repeated many times, recognizes that the television screen is McDonald's. She knows that Chad sees hamburgers and french fries as the ultimate meal. It is a good way to start each morning, driving to McDonald's and making your wishes come true.

When preschool children playact, all their wishes can be realized. Any day can be a holiday or a vacation. There are no rules like "eat your dinner before dessert," no restrictions like "that's too expensive," no excuses like "we don't have time now."

The tea party, which probably has been handed down for centuries, is the prototype of this wish fulfillment. The current tea party is more likely to be a coffee break or a birthday celebration, but the message is still the same: "Let's have a party." During the preschool years, it is interesting to watch children expand their party scripts. Laura started off serving roast beef and plum pie at her tea parties. Gradually the parties became more formalized and the preparations more elaborate. "Have to catch a fish," she muttered more to herself than to her mother, who was sitting on a quilt that turned out to be the ocean. Laura caught the fish, then got out pots and pans to cook the fish "with sauce." "Be careful of the steam," she cautioned her mother. Then she set the table by arranging play dishes on a pillow. Placing a block on a coaster, Laura added this "candle" to the pillow table. "Would you like dinner music?" she asked her mother. "I'll turn the music and TV on." Finally it was time to eat the fish and broccoli—plus sandwiches (in case someone didn't like fish and broccoli). After dinner, Laura washed the dishes by pretending that a cabinet knob was a faucet, dried them with a towel, and blew out the candle.

As preschool children play out their favorite wish-fulfillment scenes, they demonstrate their ability to grasp sequential order. They learn to properly order events from beginning to end and to add new events in the right place. If an event was not satisfactory in real life, it can be changed in pretending. On the way to Disneyworld, Mandy's family once ran out of gas on the highway. As she replayed the trip, Mandy made sure this problem did not recur. "We go to Disneyworld," she told her dolls, "but first we need gas." Driving her imaginary van down the road, Mandy discussed other changes that would take place on this visit to Disneyworld:

> We're going to see Small World.
>
> We're going to ride the horses and ride Dumbo.
>
> We're not going to Haunted Mansion. It's too scary. Those ghosts scare me.

As Mandy played and replayed this Disneyworld theme, she reexperienced the good part of her trip and obliterated the bad part.

Power and Protection

Obviously preschool children feel powerful when their play allows them to act out parental roles, take control of the future, and make their wishes come true. The wish to be grown-up and the desire to feel powerful come together in the occupational roles they play. Not understanding occupations very well, the children often focus on such generic adult tasks as driving or shopping. In fact, if there are any pretend scenes that rival the tea party in popularity, they are the imaginary ride and the shopping spree.

Vehicles are the most prominent machines in our society, and to be in control of them is a clear sign of power. Similarly, money is a highly visible symbol of power, for the person who possesses it can obtain virtually anything. For these reasons, preschool children mark their imaginary rides by dramatic engine and siren sounds, and their shopping sprees by a never-ending flow of money. The roles of both driver and shopper are broad and filled with many possibilities. Preschool children become bus and taxi drivers, train engineers, airplane pilots, heavy equipment operators, ambulance workers, along with other variations.

Those who are interested in shopping incorporate their favorite props into buying and selling fantasies. A child who likes to dress up enjoys shopping in clothing and jewelry stores, a child who likes to pretend-cook goes to the grocery store or runs a restaurant. With the help of parents, the whole house may become a shopping mall, with dishes and food for sale in the kitchen, toys and clothes in the bedroom, and furniture in the living room.

In their driving and shopping routines, children become aware of the relative power of different roles. The provider of services, they discover, is more powerful than the person who is being served. Instead of being the buyer in a shopping routine, they choose the role of seller. Instead of being a passenger on an airplane ride, they select the role of pilot. Naturally, once they assume the pilot role, they have to recruit the passengers. "Everybody on the balloon ride," Brad announced, holding a balloon he had brought back from the circus. "See, there's a little basket under here where the people sit," he explained to his mother. Having justified his role and having warned the people about falling out, Brad proceeded to race around the room with the balloon.

The power of an occupational role is also magnified when it provides protection for other people. In this light, preschool children are drawn to roles like doctor, police officer, and fire fighter:

Terry: The people are trapped in the fire.

Father: Should we try to rescue them?

Terry: I'm crawling in the fire.

Father: What are we going to do?

Terry: Put them in the ambulance. I'm taking them to the hospital.

Father: What will we do next?

Terry: Well, we have the dog out and the mommy and the daddy.

Father: Could we go back to the station and have a cold beer?

There is something ominous, though, about the image of these heroes. Fire fighters break buildings with axes, police officers carry guns, and doctors poke needles into their patients. In their pretending, preschool children often mix violent and protective behaviors, indicating that they see the dual nature of these roles. Pretend police officers keep the peace by shooting indiscriminantly, while pretend doctors give alarming checkups. "Hold very, very still," Luis said to Scott as he brandished a toy hypodermic. "I have to give you a shot in the eye." Scott rolled his eyes in worried anticipation—wasn't this supposed to be a routine checkup? "All done," Luis concluded cheerfully. "Here's a little pink pill. You want to be the doctor?"

To some extent the children may be copying roles they see on TV, where police officers are constantly engaged in gun battles and doctors in radical surgery. Beyond this imitation, however, the children are trying to cope with genuine fears. Doctors and police, even fire fighters with their gas masks, are scary people. Pretending to be one of these characters provides not only a sense of power over others, but a feeling of power over your own fears. Police officers and doctors seem less scary if you've already been one yourself.

The dynamic involved in this kind of pretending is magical. Fear is magically reduced by taking on the scary role. Children use a similar coping strategy when they act out the role of fantasy power figures. Specific names change from Superman to HeMan but the function of all superheroes is to help children cope with fears. Superheroes are good monsters just the way police officers are the good guys with the shotguns. They have incredible powers that are used only for good purposes. They can combat the wickedness of any evil monster, giant, werewolf, witch, or robot and can protect you from dangerous criminals, storms, darkness, or wild animals.

The things that children are afraid of are sometimes real and sometimes

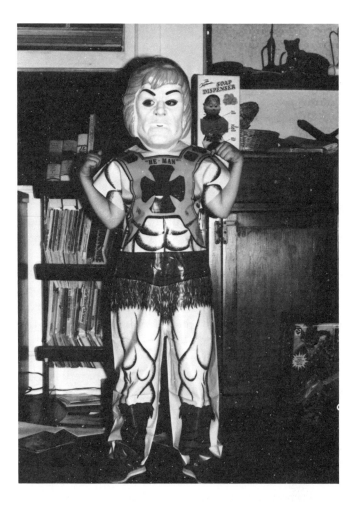

imagined. Pretending to be a power figure helps children cope with their fears no matter what the source. At the same time parents who tune in to their children's pretending can help their children talk about their fears and distinguish between real and pretend.

In the following explanation by Todd, who is pretending to be Spiderman, we can see how identifying with a power figure reveals a child's fears and opens the way for the child to separate the imaginary dangers from the real ones:

> Spiderman is not scared of anything. He's not scared of fire at all. He's not scared of water at all. He's not afraid of noise bombs. And he's not afraid of spiders and kisses.

Suggestions for Parents

One way parents can support playacting is to allow their furniture to be used as stage props. Although some preschool children select a back room, porch, or out-of-the-way spot for role-playing, most children gravitate toward central pieces of furniture. Laura had her "riding couch," which served as an all-purpose vehicle. Chad chose a large armchair in the living room, which at various times was a fire station or a fort. Older preschool children are likely to create their own space for imaginary play by rearranging pillows or draping sheets over tables. Naturally this kind of play messes up the room and increases the chance of damage. Some families reach a compromise by providing their children with a large cardboard box or by helping their child identify a "pretend corner."

Another way that parents can support playacting is by helping children find props. While too many props can overwhelm a child or stifle pretending, one or two well-selected props introduced during a lull in the action can spark additional play. When explorer Jonathan had hunted down all the lions in the family room, his mother gave him a sieve so that he could pan for gold. A bag of junk jewelry added new zest to Casandra's shopping expedition. For children who like to use particular sets of props to act out favorite themes, parents might want to provide "prop boxes" for storing each set of props. Although children eventually mix up their props (the ballet dancer might go shopping or the doctor might go out to a restaurant), the prop box helps with the problem of rounding up the appropriate supplies.

Nearly all preschool children enjoy having their parents participate in playacting. Young children who are just beginning to elaborate their pretend play welcome their parents' ability to add appropriate dialogue or extend a play idea. Older preschool children are delighted with their parents' talent for adding excitement or novelty to a standard theme.

Seth and Marvin were sailing around the living room on the sofa pillow gathering up sunken treasure. Seth's father sat down on a pillow beside them. "Oh, a pirate's life is just for me. I'll hide my treasure here in the sea, and if any boys go after it, I'll eat them for my dinner." For the next half hour, Seth and Marvin worked out secret ways of making off with the pirate's hidden treasure.

When parents join their child's pretend themes, the trick is to participate in the play without taking it over. Adults enjoy exercising their own creativity and can get carried away. Although children enjoy a playful parent, they also need to work out their own ideas. The parent who has thought up a great idea

for turning the kitchen table into a checkout counter may be less enthusiastic about moving the same three cans in and out of the shopping cart over and over again. Another problem arises when the child gets an idea that the parent feels is illogical, such as a stop off at the ocean on the way to the moon. At these points, the parent has to either accept the child's idea or find a graceful way of exiting from the play. The parent stuck in the grocery store might suggest, for instance, that the child continue with the shopping while he goes home to get more money.

Perhaps the simplest way to support playacting is to be the audience. When children are pretending to be entertainers, an audience is a necessity. At other times, preschool children do not require an audience, but they generally enjoy having one. Playacting is not very secretive at this age. An occasional question, or even a smile, lets children know that you are watching and admiring what they are doing. Parents who enjoy taking pictures can capture their children's pretending on film. Children can look back at the photos and reflect on the way they played out a theme.

Whether supporting a child's pretending actively or passively, parents have an opportunity to communicate their values. Drew's mother used pretending to demonstrate compromise. She and Drew disagreed about the necessity of Drew taking an afternoon nap. When Drew suggested that he was a dog and he wanted to nap underneath the crib, his mother provided the necessary pillow and blanket. Jackie's mother found a chance to support compassion and kindness in her daughter's doll play. When Jackie punished the doll too harshly, her mother spoke for the doll, "Please be more gentle, I promise I'll do better, Mommy." David's dad turned his son's gun play into a cooperative adventure. Instead of shooting at each other, the two of them built an elaborate trap out of rope and "poison" in order to catch the bloodthirsty dinosaur who was

terrorizing the neighborhood. Because playacting replicates human interaction, it is a fine medium for moral instruction in whatever values parents choose to introduce and reinforce.

Playacting reaches its highpoint during the preschool years. Whether children are playing alone, with a friend, or with a group, their most sustained play is likely to revolve around acting. This intense engagement of children in playacting accentuates the importance of the parent's role. Parents can foster their child's creativity and participate in his or her private world by providing the appropriate play space and props, by joining in the play, or by taking the part of appreciative audience.

Chapter 8
STORYTELLING

THE LAND OF STORY BOOKS

So when my nurse comes in for me
Home I return across the sea
and go to bed with backward looks
at my dear land of Story Books.
—ROBERT LOUIS STEVENSON

Kenneth was spending the night with his grandmother. After reading three storybooks that Kenneth had selected, she decided to put out the light. "But, Nana," Kenneth pleaded, "you promised to tell me a story."

Although reading a book to a child takes less effort than telling a story, it is never quite the same. Stories invented for the child and told in our own words create feelings of closeness and intimacy that a storybook reading can't match. Parents who spend the extra moments to tell their child a bedtime story are well rewarded. As they share fantasies and wishes with their children, they strengthen the parent-child bond and store up special memories that they will always treasure.

Listening to Stories

Because the role of storyteller is a difficult one, it is natural for young children to concentrate initially on the role of listener. Learning to appreciate a story, in fact, is a considerable challenge for preschool children. For younger preschool children, the challenge lies in making connections between the spoken words and illustrations and in following the story line. Older preschool children become increasingly involved in more subtle aspects of the story, like the motivation of the characters or the consequences of an event. Why did Peter Rabbit go into the garden? What will happen if he does it again?

Whatever its complexity, the attraction of a story is its power to arouse emotions. The imaginary action of a story can trigger many different emotions, however, certain themes recur in the stories that appeal to young children. By far the most common theme is individual achievement: the solution of a problem, the completion of an adventure, or the accomplishment of some goal. Feelings engendered by such stories include excitement, pride, and confidence.

Many fairy tales and traditional stories are of this type. Preschool children are particularly attracted to fairy tales in which children, or childlike characters, save themselves from a monster. On the surface, these stories involve common people and animals in ordinary settings. The initial atmosphere actually seems banal, but out of this deceptive calm a monster character appears.

Three kinds of monsters are prominent all of whom are distorted versions of familiar family members. There are wild-animal monsters, such as the wolf in *Little Red Riding Hood* or *The Three Little Pigs.* The wolf, who looks like a pet dog, is really evil and vicious. Then there are father monsters, men whose size has gotten out of hand and turned into brutality. They are giants. Finally, mothers can become monsters too. Their noses get long and knobby, they wear ugly clothes, and they surround themselves with bugs, frogs, and bats. Worst of all, their cooking is poisonous. Instead of nurturing children, they cast evil spells on them. Mother monsters are witches.

Monster stories have great emotional appeal for preschool children because they speak to real fears. The children are concerned about being attacked by animals with sharp teeth or being threatened by angry and malevolent parents. Feeling strong enough to protect yourself, through the vicarious experience of a story, is reassuring.

Many fairy tales also involve a contrast between wisdom and foolishness. In *Little Red Riding Hood,* for example, the wolf absurdly thinks that by putting on the grandmother's clothes, he can fool the little girl. Such silliness, exaggeration, and logical absurdity play a part in most stories that appeal to young children. Preschool children can recognize such foolishness, eliciting feelings of delight and superiority, emotions that complement but are distinct from feelings of excitement and pride. Among traditional stories, the Mother Goose Rhymes are the purest examples of this theme. The silliness of made-up words is combined with impossible events:

Hey diddle, diddle,

The cat and the fiddle,

The cow jumped over the moon,

The little dog laughed

To see such sport,

And the dish ran away with the spoon.

Current authors, such as Dr. Seuss, succeed in bringing forth the same kind of feelings in a modern context.

In recent years, a third theme has become more noticeable. Many stories are focusing on feelings that are part of intimate relationships. There are stories about making and losing friends, about feeling sad when someone dies, about feeling jealous of a new baby. Preschool children are interested in exploring these feelings by listening to stories. Their desire to empathize with others and to be caring is stimulated.

Good stories tend to produce a variety of feelings in both adults and children. Such stories, like people, are emotionally complex. Parents and children can explore their feelings of accomplishment, amusement, and empathy when they share these stories.

First Attempts at Storytelling

When preschool children begin to recite a favorite story word for word, turning the pages at just the right moment, they are indicating that they want to assume the role of storyteller. Although their performance is not true storytelling, it does help them become aware of how stories are structured. Stories have their own logic in which the characters are developed, the central problem is resolved, and a final theme emerges. There are many variations, of course, on this basic story structure, but until children have internalized these elements they cannot tell coherent stories.

When children go beyond memorization and describe what they see happening in the pictures of a book, they are coming closer to storytelling. Typically, however, these descriptions do not add up to a unified story line. Children may begin with comments that connect the first few pictures, but then they suddenly switch focus and pick up another idea. Similarly, preschool children make up charming songs and monologues that include connected images but not a coherent story line. Listen to Mandy, sitting in the sandbox and singing a song about toes:

When I take off my shoes,

I wiggle them like a worm.

My toes are saying gobble, gobble.

They are a turkey, like a bunny—

See those two little ears.

This is Mickey Mouse

And he wiggles like a worm.

Mickey Mouse, with his big fat ears,

And his face is round.

And he wiggles like a worm.

The most polished stories are told by children as they pretend with small-scale toys. We call this kind of storytelling "producer-director" play. Like the producer-director of a film or drama, the children tell the story by controlling the actions of a cast of characters. The cast may be tiny dolls, transformer robots, toy animals, or even miniature cars. Assuming the detached perspective of the producer-director, the children animate the characters by speaking for them and narrating the action:

Here comes Sound Waves—*hiss-hiss-hiss.* The Deceptagons are coming down to earth. Rumbles and Ravage are on the loose. *Swish-swish*—they are getting the energy cubes. Watch out—the earth is blowing up. Oh, no you don't. Prime to the rescue. Open up the battle station. Bumblebee on the attack-*tat-tat-tat-a-tat.* They opened fire. They are turning around. They are back in Cybetron. The earth is saved. Hurray for Prime! Hurray for Bumblebee!

In producer-director play, theatrical devices help children tell the story. It is not necessary to describe the story's setting, for it is apparent from the arrangement of toys. As the characters speak, the producer/director moves them up and down, thereby eliminating the need for phrases like "she said" or "he asked." Likewise, transitions between events can be demonstrated by manipulating the toys rather than through narration. The children are free to concentrate on the dialogue, and when two children work together, each one taking a different role, the dialogue can carry a recognizable story line:

Gina (Holding a Mickey Mouse character): Hello, Donald. Ready for the Mickey Mouse Revue?

Karen (Holding Donald Duck): No, I can't come, I lost my drumstick.

Gina: Well, you better find it. The parade has got to get started.

Karen: The dragon eated it up.

Gina: You got bad trouble!

Preschool children who have a special gift for storytelling may progress to the point of producing original stories without props. Even then, however, their stories are more like a series of snapshots than a continuous flow of events. Brian, after a hurricane warning, told the following original story:

> There was a hurricane over the house. A hand came down and picked Brian up by the hair. He cut the hand off, and it fell to the ground. He took the hand to jail.

More commonly, preschool children show they are on their way to original storytelling by adding a new bit to a familiar story. Celia created an original version of *Goldilocks and the Three Bears:*

> Then Goldilocks took a bite of Momma Bear's porridge. She said, "This is too yucky!" and she ran out of the bear's house and her mommy took her to McDonald's and all the bears went home, and momma bear said "Who ate my porridge?" The end.

Like other kinds of imaginative play, the stories a child tells, whatever the form, reveal that child's feelings. By watching and listening we can glimpse their wishes, fears, and joyfulness. Brennan, at five years old, is celebrating a sunny day:

> It's not the leaves.
>
> It's not the rakes.
>
> It's the sun of the morn.
>
> Just don't put on your sunglasses
>
> Just go out into the sun of the morn.
>
> Just play in the leaves
>
> Your father raked for you.
>
> It's fun in the sun of the morn.

The Extra Storyteller

Television is the extra storyteller in every family, and its versatility is growing with the appearance of cable channels and video cassettes. Children are exposed to an overwhelming number of stories through television. This form of storytelling has the disadvantage of being less controlled by the children. They cannot stop and talk about part of a story nor skip a scary event. Often they cannot even watch the show again. On the other hand, television storytelling can be exceptionally powerful as far as arousing emotion. Because it is a visual medium in which close-ups of the human face appear constantly the viewer's attention is directed toward body language and facial expression.

Research studies clearly indicate that television viewing influences the attitudes of young children. Watching violent programming results in more aggressive play and, presumably, a more accepting attitude toward violence. By contrast, watching programs about minority or handicapped children or about foreign countries results in a more accepting attitude toward differences in people.

At the same time, research also indicates that preschool children do not attend to televised information in a consistent or efficient fashion. Younger preschool children look away from the screen much of the time. Older preschool children, who watch more steadily, do not seem to be organizing information into scenes. When asked to recall what happened in a program, they do not remember events in detail or in the proper order. Apparently they have not picked up implied information or understood the motivation of the characters.

The overall picture that emerges from these studies is that young children do not really understand what is going on in most television programs but that they pick up general attitudes by watching. Another way of saying it is that the children notice the feelings of the characters without understanding the motivation for their actions. At this point, we cannot be sure what kind of television storytelling is most appropriate for preschool children. It is unrealistic to expect them to understand shows that are produced for teenagers and adults, just as they do not comprehend books written for older people. The success of *Sesame Street* on the other hand, suggests that young children can appreciate television stories under certain circumstances.

Over the years, children have responded with enthusiasm to *Sesame Street*'s Muppets and other characters, like Big Bird, who dramatically express their feelings. The characters are visually interesting "animals" and the segments are short, which helps keep the children's attention. The scenes are repeated many times, which enables the children to recognize the different personalities and appreciate their characteristic emotions. Children learn to anticipate that Cookie Monster will be good-naturedly greedy, Grover will announce in a tremulous voice how powerful he is, and so forth.

Although these Muppet scenes are generally designed to reinforce academic concepts, it seems reasonable to suppose that preschool children could appreciate similar characters in a variety of story adventures. In fact, television, because it can present human emotions so powerfully, seems ideally suited to stimulate children's thinking about character motivation. There is a great deal of potential to create more television stories that match the interest and attention span of preschool children.

Suggestions for Parents

Since storytelling begins with listening, parents can help their children get started by reading them interesting books. Most public libraries have large collections of picture books with suitable stories for preschoolers. If possible, it is a good idea to plan on at least half an hour of browsing in order to select the ones you really like. Preschool children usually grab the first books they see, which can result in dull or inappropriate stories. Let your child pick a few books and then look at them in the library while you select additional books more carefully. A children's librarian can be very helpful in suggesting particular authors and illustrators.

In choosing books for your child, think about the following qualities:

- How well is the book illustrated? Children enjoy looking at pictures as much as listening to words. They enjoy beauty, humor, and fantasy. Avoid books where the illustrations are too busy or overstylized.

- Does the book match my child's listening skills? Do not go by age. Choose a story that is complex enough to capture your child's interest but easy enough to follow.

- Is this a book that my child will enjoy? Don't be overconcerned with educational value. Any story that your child enjoys is educationally valid.

- Does the story have emotional appeal? Although children enjoy informational books, books that qualify as long time favorites appeal to a child's emotions.

- Is the book well written? Children tune into the sound of language as well as its meaning. Be especially wary of books that are marked "easy reading." They may be easy to read, but very dull to listen to.

- Does the book appeal to you? When you read a book to your child that you really like, the chances are very good that your child will like it too.

What if your child isn't interested in books and won't sit still to listen to a story? Here are three ways to approach the problem:

- Stimulate the child's interest in pictures. Most books for young children have many pictures, and if your child becomes sufficiently interested in the pictures, listening to the stories will follow naturally. Find out which pictures attract your child and talk about them. Pictures are everywhere, in books, painting, posters, billboards, signs, photographs. Perhaps your child would like more activity—cut and paste pictures from magazines.

- Tantalize your child with reading. Choose a book you think will interest your child, sit down alone, and read the book loudly to yourself. Be sure to sit in a spot that is convenient for the child to join you.

- Try the appeal of high-tech reading. Buy a book with an accompanying cassette tape and show your child how to operate the tape recorder. If your child prefers listening to stories on the tape recorder, you can easily record other picture books.

As you read storybooks, there are many opportunities to encourage your child to become an active participant, to join in the storytelling. Naturally, it is fun to pause and talk about the pictures. Look for surprises or incongruities in the pictures. Illustrators seem to enjoy adding private jokes to their pictures. Perhaps a detail you find will suggest a new twist to the plot, such as a mouse who looks sad when everyone else in the picture is happy. Try going beyond the information in the picture: "I wonder who lives in this tree? Where do you think that car is going in such a hurry?"

When reading a story for the first time, you and your child can sometimes guess what's going to come next before you turn the page. If your child likes to make guesses, stop midway through the story and try to predict how it will end. This technique, which also can be used with television programs, is an excellent way to help your child become more aware of story structure.

Because you can read the book and your child cannot, conversations about a story can sometimes seem like quizzes to the child. One way to soften your authoritative position is to use a puppet. As you read the story, the puppet breaks in with comments and questions. Conversely, your child can hold the puppet. Then your comments will be directed to a puppet who may be more willing to respond.

In your conversations about a story, remember the potential of stories to highlight human motivation. You can question a character's emotional state: "I guess she's getting madder and madder." You can compare yourself to a character: "I wouldn't do that because it's too dangerous," or invite your child to make such a comparison. You can place yourself and your child directly in the story:

"I'm not scared of that tiger; I'm going to stand on this rock—where are you going to stand?"

The purpose of all these techniques is to make story reading like storytelling. The activity becomes more fun for both you and your child as the two of you add your imaginative power to that of the author. Soon you will gain confidence in your ability to tell stories and may not need the book at all. If you still feel a bit unsure about your own storytelling, try one of these ideas:

· Tell a "story" that recaps an experience from the past. You can recount what you or your child did yesterday or retell a special event from the recent past. Change some of the details or provide a surprise ending.

- Build a story from a book that you and your child have enjoyed. Describe the further adventures of the main characters. Perhaps you can imagine them visiting your family.

- Tell a story that is based on one of your child's drawings. Think about the objects your child likes to draw and weave them into a story.

As you experiment with storytelling, involve your child in the process. Preschool children enjoy defining the characters: thinking up names for them, deciding whether they live in a big house or a little house, and so on. At the end, they like to choose a happy ending or a sad ending.

You can also help your child tell a story through producer-director play. You can encourage the play to start by asking your child to tell you the names of the characters (whether they are miniature dolls, toy robots, or some other kind of toy). You can ask what the characters are going to do or suggest that one of the characters wants to do a particular thing. You can even assume a role and help create the dialogue.

Producer-director play is a transitional step between playacting and storytelling. One way to help your child see this connection is to write down what happens during the play. Although you may not be able to hear all the dialogue or write fast enough to keep up, you can record the main action and ideas, then

edit it into a compact story and read it to your child. Older preschool children, who no longer want parents to participate directly in their imaginative play, may appreciate this kind of support. A permanent record of producer-director play demonstrates very clearly that they are becoming real storytellers.

During the preschool years, storytelling is a form of imaginative play that is handed down from parent to child. Typically, the parents read books to their children until gradually the children begin "reading" the books themselves. In our concern to prepare young children for reading, we can lose sight of story-telling as the larger context. The purpose for reading picture books is to experience on an imaginative level the emotions of the characters in the story. Our imaginations are further involved when we retell and elaborate the stories of others or make up our own stories from scratch. Ultimately, we give our children the best start when we help them see that the source for all stories, whether they come from a book, television, or personal experience, is imaginative thinking.

By the end of the preschool period, children have learned to draw, to build, and to role-play without adult assistance. Storytelling, being a more abstract form of imaginative play, is slower to develop. Stories are acted out in producer-director play, but true storytelling is sporadic. Instead, children listen to stories and learn how they are put together. They enjoy talking about the details of stories and imagining possible variations. With the help of parents, they are building a foundation for storytelling that is still to come.

Part IV
PLAYING WITH LETTERS AND NUMBERS

During preschool orientation, day Miss Becky gave each child a paper Care Bear with his or her name on it to tape under the Care Bear tree. "After today," Miss Becky explained, "you will come to school without your mommy and your Care Bear will watch out for you." When orientation was over, Laura convinced her teacher to give her an extra Care Bear. With the help of the school secretary, she wrote her nana's name on the Care Bear and stuck it under the tree in the classroom. On the way out she told her mother, "Nana is coming to school with me. I put her name under the tree." Laura at three years old, like other preschool children, ascribed a certain magic power to numbers and letters. Nana's name on the bulletin board could beckon the real person to the classroom and take away the scariness of the first day of school.

In this section, we look at children's natural fascination with letters and numbers and describe how this interest in "adult" symbols can provide the impetus for learning academic skills. In each of the chapters, we will see that reading, writing, and arithmetic, like other preschool skills, are learned in an effortless way through play and conversation.

This section, "Play with Letters and Numbers" consists of two chapters. Chapter 9 looks at ways in which children play at reading and writing and sometimes actually learn to read. Chapter 10 focuses on quantitative thinking and describes the sequence of counting skills that children are likely to acquire. In the suggestions for parents at the end of each chapter, we discuss ways to support a child's spontaneous interest in reading, writing, and counting while maintaining the spirit of fun and adventure.

Chapter 9
READING AND WRITING

ELECTEPHONY

Once there was an elephant
Who tried to use the telephant—
No! No! I mean an elephone
Who tried to use the telephone
(Dear me! I am not certain quite
That even now I've got it right.)

Howe'er it was, he got his trunk
Entangled in the telephunk:
The more he tried to get it free
The louder buzzed the telephee.
(I fear I'd better drop the song
Of elephop and telephong!)

—Laura E. Richards

Tami, at three years old, was a regular fan of *Sesame Street.* She loved watching the letters of the alphabet pop onto the screen and could name almost every one. Two years later, when Tami entered kindergarten, she was reading books. Tami's parents were convinced that her precocious reading could be attributed to *Sesame Street.*

However, Tami's story is not necessarily typical. Children who learn to name letters at an early age will not necessarily read early. Some children do make steady progress from naming letters to sounding out words to reading books, but for most children this progression is neither quick nor steady. Fortunately, with few exceptions, children who have good language skills and who enjoy having books read to them will become good readers in elementary school. On the other hand, children who are drilled in reading before they show a spontaneous interest may develop negative feelings about the skill. It is a lot more productive to teach preschool children how to enjoy books than to teach them how to read.

In this chapter, we look at ways in which children in the preschool years lay the groundwork for reading and writing. The first section focuses on children's ability to sound out and recognize words. In the second section, we examine their ability to interpret messages. In the third section, we talk about writing skills. We look at how children use their interest in written messages as a bridge to learning to read. The final section of the chapter is devoted to suggestions for parents.

Word Recognition

As the sky-writing plane passed overhead, three-year-old Brenda stared in amazement. The words, VISIT CLAM BAKERS were stretched across the horizon. "Mommy, Mommy, look, my *B* is up there!"

The sequence in which children learn words is fairly predictable. Generally, the first word they recognize is their own name and they feel quite possessive about all of its letters. Next, they are likely to turn their interest to logos. Parents have reported that their two- and three-year-olds can recognize the names of fast-food restaurants or the labels on cereal boxes. Although these young children rely on many cues other than the sequence of letters to identify these words, this spontaneous sign reading is impressive.

Parents who believe in formal reading instruction for preschoolers may introduce flash cards as a way of building sight vocabulary. Occasionally a child will really enjoy these flash cards and master an impressive stack of words. More often, children learn a word one day and forget it completely the next. Somehow learning to attach the right words to a stack of cardboard cards doesn't have the same appeal as identifying a McDonald's restaurant or finding the box of Cheerios on the pantry shelf.

While some parents use a flash-card approach to teach early word reading, other parents focus on teaching alphabet skills. They may begin by teaching their child to name and identify the letters of the alphabet, or they may try to teach phonic skills by concentrating on the sounds that letters make. Whichever route the parent takes, there are complications. Letters make different sounds in different words, and upper-case letters look different from lower-case letters. Hal had learned to identify the letters in his name in upper case. When his aunt wrote his name in lower-case letters, Hal came running to his mother. "Do you know what Aunt Caroline did? She took the foot off my *l*!"

Even if a child is successful in learning the different sounds and shapes of all the letters, there is a long road ahead before they learn to read words. The first challenge to overcome is sound blending or stringing the sounds together. A child may sound out *c-a-t* without a flaw and still not know that the word he is sounding out is *cat*. A second problem that children face is the irregularity of the English language. The more common a word is, the less likely it is to follow phonetic rules. Think about the words in this sentence: "Two girls were in the house." Except for *in,* none of the words in this sentence can be sounded out.

Despite the many difficulties involved, some preschool children do learn enough phonics to read simple words just as some children build a sight vocabu-

lary through their exposure to flash cards. In either case, the child has learned to associate the written word with both its spoken counterpart and its meaning. Although parents are justifiably pleased when their children make this kind of breakthrough, word identification cannot be equated with reading. Reading involves the ability to extract the meaning from a complex written message.

Learning to Read Messages

There is a watershed separation between reading words and reading messages. In order to understand a written message, children must recognize how the words they read are related to each other. Even children with good phonic skills may be unable to read a complete sentence. The small words like *the* and *are* that connect the nouns and the verbs are likely to be irregular. When children try to sound them out, they lose the sense of the sentence.

Children who have learned to read by a flash card approach also have difficulty with function words but for a different reason. Four-year-old Sari, who had trouble remembering the flash card with the word *the* sheds some light on the problem. "Mommy," she asked one day, "what does a *the* look like?"

Although parents who work hard at teaching their preschool child to read are often unsuccessful, there are some preschoolers who learn to read with ease. These early readers have certain characteristics in common. They enjoy listening to stories and are good conversationalists. They have parents who enjoy reading and who provide them with a selection of attractive books. One or both parents have been available to answer questions, but they have not drilled or quizzed their child. In other words, the parents of children who are early readers have created a climate that encourages their child to read for enjoyment.

While we can say with assurance that children who read early will read well in elementary school, many children who make no attempts to read on their own until they get to first grade become excellent readers as well. With all children, the critical variable seems to be the association of pleasure with reading. Children who have learned at an early age that reading is a source of pleasure will become good readers by the time they are six or seven.

Writing and Reading

While some children are more interested than others in learning the names of letters, almost every child is fascinated by writing. In the beginning, writing is a kind of pretending. Children make some squiggles on a piece of paper and ask their parent to read what they have written. Although children know that their squiggles are not real writing, it doesn't detract from the fun of these conversational games.

Children who begin with squiggles very often go on to forming real letters. Naturally, the first letters that they form are the letters in their own name, and the first word they write is their name. Children's interest in reading and writing tends to follow the same sequence: from letters to words to messages. However, they are usually interested in writing messages before they have mastered reading books.

Children who are interested in writing messages pursue this interest in different ways. Some think up messages and ask their parents to write them out. Others laboriously write out a message by asking their parents to dictate to them one letter at a time. Once they have written out a message, they read it aloud.

Writing letters, for a preschooler, is a tedious task and quite naturally they look for shortcuts. An obvious shortcut is to begin with ready-made letters. Brenan liked to arrange plastic letters on the refrigerator door. By paying attention to the commercials on television, he discovered that letters put in order make a word. One morning, after watching a commercial, he lined up the letters *J-E-L-L-O* "I did it," he announced proudly. "I wrote *Jell-O.*"

The problem with magnetic letters, Brenan soon discovered, is that you are likely to run out of letters. A solution to the problem is a typewriter or a computer. With these marvelous grown-up toys, not only do you have an infinite supply of letters, but they come out looking perfect. In a typewritten message, the letters are always right side up and on the line in a perfect left-right sequence. Justin played a dictionary game with his dad using an electric typewriter. He and his dad would take turns finding words in the dictionary and typing them out on the typewriter. Pretty soon the game became more elaborate, and Justin typed the names and addresses of the children in his class. He put these names and addresses in the cubbies of the children at school, an early attempt at message sending.

When a computer or typewriter is not available, and sometimes even if it is, children enjoy assigning the role of scribe to their parent. Kenneth, at the

age of five, insisted that his mother include a written note with every school lunch. When he got to school, he would ask the teacher to please read him the note. Christopher, who liked to put on shows, would ask his mother to post a sign outside his door with the title of the next performance. Lauren would dictate letters to all her friends with her grandmother doing the writing.

Suggestions for Parents

From a very early age, children love to have people read to them. In some families, the practice of reading a bedtime story continues through the pre-school years. In other families, the practice peters out as parents get busy with younger siblings or children become independent about bedtime. Although parents may not want to read to their preschool children at a set time, reading to children on a daily basis is a good practice.

Although we do not recommend flash cards and commercial reading-readiness workbooks, there are many prereading games that parents and children can enjoy. Some of these games help children tune into the sound system of language. Other games capitalize on their interest in writing.

Games with Sounds

Learning to recognize rhyming words sensitizes children to differences in vowel sounds. More importantly, most children have fun with rhyming words. In addition to reading poems and rhyming books, parents and children can invent their own rhyming games.

As your child gets dressed in the morning or puts away his or her toys, invent a silly couplet and let her put in the rhyming word:

> I wonder what you're going to do.
> I think you will put on your ——.

> I see something over there.
> I think it is your teddy ——.

A second way to tune children into letter sounds is to play games with first-letter sounds. The preschool practice of having a letter of the week can be carried out at home. On *B* day, for instance, you might want to find a picture of a butterfly, let bear and Big Bird join you for breakfast, and serve beans and bacon for dinner. A less elaborate game involves making up alliteration sentences: "Susie saw a silly salamander sitting in the sun."

Games with Letters

Children are intrigued by letters and enjoy incorporating them into their games. If you have a set of alphabet blocks or magnetic letters, try writing out your child's name leaving a space for a missing letter. Your child will enjoy the challenge of finding the missing letter and putting it in place. For the child who is interested in spelling out simple words, play beginner's Draw-a-Man. Like regular Hangman, the goal of the game is to guess the letters of the word before a stick figure of a man is completed. (Every time the player guesses a letter that is not in the word, one stroke is added to the stick figure.) For beginner's Draw-a-Man, tell your child the word before the game begins. Then, when she guesses a letter that is in the word, place the letter in the correct spot on the word line.

Writing Messages

Once your child is familiar with the way letters look and sound, he or she is likely to become interested in reading and writing messages. Children who like

to write enjoy sending out short letters and party invitations, exchanging notes with a parent, or making up shopping lists. (Don't correct their spelling! It takes the fun out of writing.) For children who are more interested in reading messages, ask them to describe their drawings and write out the description, tack messages on the refrigerator, put a short note in their lunch box, or play a treasure-hunt game using word clues.

Preschool is an important time for building the foundation for reading. This foundation includes a familiarity with the sounds and letters of the alphabet, an awareness that reading and writing are ways of communicating messages, and an ability to follow a story. Above all, a foundation for reading includes a desire to read and a willingness to try. When parents are overanxious about their children's reading and push them to read before they are ready, children resist reading lessons and associate reading with failure. When parents, on the other hand, are relaxed about their children's reading and admire their spontaneous efforts without quizzing or overcorrecting, their children associate reading with pleasure and success. If a child is convinced that someday he or she will be a good reader, this conviction is almost certain to be a self-fulfilling prophecy.

Chapter 10
NUMBERS

Baa, baa, black sheep
  Have you any wool?
Yes, sir, yes, sir,
  Three bags full;
One for the master
  And one for the dame,
And one for the little boy
  Who lives down the lane.

Rachel: One, two, three, five, seven: Here I come, ready or not—

Kenneth: No Rachel, count one, two, three, four, five. Then you say, Here I come, ready or not.

Rachel: (imitating her brother's intonation): One, two, three, five, seven: Here I come, ready or not.

Rachel was attracted to the idea of counting, but despite her brother's careful tutoring, she couldn't reproduce the correct sequence. Like Rachel, most three-year-olds recite numbers in some sort of order, but they tend to skip over a number or two or say some numbers out of order. Counting by rote, which is emphasized by parents and preschool teachers alike, is only one part of the quantitative understanding that children acquire during the preschool period. During these years, children also learn to recognize sets and count rationally. They learn the meaning of comparative terms: more, same as, less, bigger, stronger, and faster. Some preschool children with a fascination for numbers learn to add and subtract as well.

Development of Rational Counting

Jennifer, at two years old, liked to create a Disneyworld parade with her blocks and toy zoo animals. She would make a row of blocks and line up three animals on each block. Like Jennifer, many young children show an awareness of sets before they begin to count systematically. Gradually, small sets are associated with numbers. The children learn that they have two eyes, two hands, and two feet. Perhaps they learn that there are five fingers on each hand and five toes on each foot or that a dog has four feet and a car has four wheels.

At the same time, very young children start paying attention to the number sequence. Mark's favorite way of being carried to bed was on his father's shoulders. Every night, his father recited the same rhyme:

One, two, three, four.
Here we are at Markie's door.
Five, six, seven, eight.
Go to sleep. It's getting late.

Before long, Mark was counting for his teddy bear as he carried him on his shoulders to bed.

By the beginning of the preschool period, these two early accomplishments, set recognition and rote counting, are starting to come together. Most three-year-olds realize that the number sequence is used to count the quantity in a set. Counting accurately is a different matter. A child who counts only to five cannot accurately count ten objects. Accuracy is further diminished when numbers are skipped or out of order. Most fundamentally, counting cannot be accurate until a child assigns one and only one number to each object in a set. The principle of one-to-one correspondence is the basis for rational counting.

In trying to count a set of objects, young preschoolers usually show a general appreciation of one-to-one correspondence but not a precise understanding. Children move their fingers from one object to another and recite the number sequence; in general they recite one number for each object. But from time to time, they will assign two numbers to a single object or pass over an object altogether. They either don't notice this lack of consistency or consider

it to be of little consequence. The bottom line is that the children's final answers are often "about right" rather than exactly right.

The most likely points for error are at the beginning and end of a counting activity. In the beginning, children need to establish a common rhythm between their verbal counting and their finger movement. If adults help them count the first few items accurately, the children may be able to continue synchronized counting and pointing. Further difficulty may arise, however, if the objects are in a circular or scattered pattern. Quite often the children forget where they started and stop prematurely, or else count some objects for a second time.

By the end of the preschool period, most children understand one-to-one correspondence precisely enough to count small sets of objects accurately. They also can make two sets equal. "You have three cookies," Marcus' mother told him. "Your sister only has two. How many more cookies does she need so both of you will have the same?" Although this kind of question requires nothing more than counting, it assumes the form of an addition problem. Without being aware of it, Marcus is exploring the fact that $2 + 1 = 3$. Preschool children who can count accurately are ready for other counting activities that involve addition and subtraction. "Four people will be eating dinner. I put one fork on the table already. How many more should I get?"

Despite preschool children's increased skill, counting generally remains a rigid routine rather than a logical system they can decipher. Meredith, a five-year-old who loved to count, tried one day to count the number of stairs to her bedroom. Interrupted when she was nearly at the top, she came back down the stairs and started with "one." At first her parents interpreted this behavior as a clever stalling tactic, but later they noticed the same thing happening in other situations. Even if they tried to help by reminding her where she left off, Meredith could not pick up a counting sequence in the middle. Numbers were not yet a logical system that could be accessed at various points.

Even when five-year-olds become adept at counting, they can make mistakes that are surprising to adults. Having agreed that two rows have ten pennies each, and therefore the same amount, a child may change his or her answer when one row is spread out or bunched together. The two rows of pennies no longer look alike, and the child jumps to the conclusion that they no longer have the same number of pennies. If the problem is simplified by using one set of objects, similar results are likely. First, the child counts the line of pennies and gives the correct answer, "Ten." Then the pennies are placed in a stack, which looks quite different from the line, and the child is asked how many pennies there are now. Instead of answering immediately (no pennies have been added or removed), the child counts the stack of pennies all over again.

The realization that quantity is independent from appearance is called number conservation. Most preschoolers, even those who are good counters, have difficulty with number conservation.

Timothy arranged his toy cars in a row and counted them one by one. "I have ten cars," he announced proudly. His father, who was curious about his son's knowledge of numbers, pushed the cars together and challenged his son to recount. Timothy scowled at his father. "Why did you do that? Now I don't got ten anymore."

Once children develop a meaningful number system, they can count a set starting with a number higher than one and they know that the number of objects in a set stays the same when the set is rearranged. They also discover that they can figure out number problems without using any objects at all. This "magic" is accomplished by double counting. The easiest kind of problem seems to be of the following type: If you need ten pennies to buy a balloon but have only seven, how many more pennies do you need? The children start counting at seven and count eight, nine, ten with one part of their brain while counting one, two, three with another part. Eight means one more, nine means two more, and ten means three more. Counting on your fingers, children learn very quickly, makes this double-counting task easier.

Once children develop this internalized double-counting system, simple story problems are welcome. They give children a chance to demonstrate their amazing new powers. Although preschool children often do not reach this level of insight, many of them are on the verge of it and will become "mathematical magicians" in the next year or two. It is an exciting period for both parents and children.

Higher Rote Counting

Rote counting, which usually precedes and therefore stimulates rational counting, continues to develop during the preschool years. Children generally have adopted the correct number sequence from one to ten by the age of four. There are so many opportunities to hear and use these numbers that they learn the sequence almost effortlessly.

Learning the sequence from ten to twenty represents a second milestone in rote counting. Preschool children often go through a period in which their counting system seems stuck somewhere between these two numbers. For one thing, there are fewer finger games, nursery rhymes, and songs that encourage children to practice this sequence. There are also new number words to learn —eleven, twelve, and the strange addition of "teen" suffixes. Many children learn this sequence gradually as adults help them apply their rational counting skills to larger sets of objects. By the end of the preschool period, most children have mastered, or are close to mastering, this second milestone.

The numbers from twenty to one hundred constitute a third level of rote counting. They are not such common numbers that they are effortlessly absorbed by children, but neither do they include as many new and unfamiliar terms as the sequence from ten to twenty. Kori had been counting steps on a walk with her grandmother. Her counting was flawless until she reached twenty-nine. "Nana," she asked, stopping dead in her tracks, "does 'three-ty' come after twenty-nine?"

Except for the fact that each decade has a new name, the numbers from twenty to one hundred flow in a predictable order. Before this regularity is apparent, however, it may be necessary to unlearn the pattern that was established between ten and twenty, where the term for the decade, "teen," was at the end of the number instead of the beginning. As easy as the sequence is from twenty to one hundred, there is little reason to recite it, until children do get caught up in the regularity of the pattern. Then the children become excited by the idea that the one to ten sequence is expandable. They get their first glimpse of the idea that numbers go on and on.

As preschool children practice counting beyond twenty, they pay special attention to conversations in which these numbers are mentioned. Children hear that Uncle Phillip is thirty-eight, that Grandpa is sixty-two, and that Great-grandma Minnie (who is very, very old) is eighty-eight. Over time, conversations like these help children understand the relative value associated with higher numbers.

With the advent of digital clocks, higher numbers have achieved new visual prominence. Of course, before preschool children can appreciate numbers in this form, they must learn the basic numerals. Recognizing the numerals one to nine generally occurs a bit later than rote counting, although *Sesame Street* alerts many young children to these symbols. Drew, for example, began to look for the numeral six, because that was Bert's favorite number. Soon he also was looking for three, his mom's favorite numeral, and ten, which he liked. Preschool children are drawn to numerals on push-button telephones, hand calculators, electric typewriters, and home computers. As they link the numerals with familiar number words, the stage is set for visual recognition of higher numbers.

Justin, a four-year-old, carefully watched the digital clock that was built into the television. He had learned from experience that when the clock said 8:00, his favorite cartoon would be shown. Watching in anticipation as the seconds flashed by, Justin began to recognize the patterns from 00 to 59. When he found these same numbers on the microwave (in reverse order), his interest increased still further. Justin's mother showed him how to punch in a certain number of seconds on the microwave. With practice, he learned many of the two-digit numerals between ten and sixty. At the same time, Justin became aware that these numbers were used to label houses. His house was 1451, and eventually he learned to type the complete address on the family's electric typewriter. Justin's interest in higher numbers was greater than average, but it illustrates the kind of experience that can stimulate rote counting from twenty to one hundred.

Measurement

Preschool children have a marvelous time going around the house with a yard-stick pretending to measure everything, however, they usually are not ready to grasp the concept of measurement. Measurement is a complex form of counting in which continuous units, rather than objects, are counted. Moreover, the units are, to all appearances, arbitrary. There is no discernable reason why length is measured in inches or weight in pounds.

Whatever the given unit, the secret to accurate measurement is keeping that unit consistent. It is this principle that is beyond the understanding of preschool children. Given a cardboard footprint that is twelve inches long, they will be happy to measure how many "feet" it is from the kitchen to the bathroom. Of course, they will be unconcerned about carefully lining up the footprint so that each measured unit is equal. In effect, the children will treat the activity as one in which a series of footprints are counted, for that is the kind of counting they understand.

Despite their inability to measure accurately, preschool children are learning three basic ideas about measurement. First, they are learning comparative terms that are used to measure things in a perceptual, nonquantitative manner.

Many preschool children develop a rich vocabulary of these terms: bigger/smaller, longer/shorter, faster/slower, older/younger, heavier/lighter.

Second, the children are learning to associate the names of certain units with the attributes that they measure. The children become aware that pounds refer to weight, inches to length, and miles per hour to speed. This process of association is not without its comic side:

Candice (As cashier):	You gotta put your stuff up here so I can ring it up. This is going to cost you lots of money.
Mother (As customer):	Don't forget to weigh the apples.
Candice:	I did. They weigh fifteen cents.

Third, children are learning to associate numbers with units of measurement. Allen's understanding of weight was superficial, but he knew that he weighed fifty-two pounds. In the same way, Sherry knew her mom was thirty-four years old even though the duration of a year was obscure. Davita found out that the speed limit in town was thirty miles per hour, and that her parents drove sixty miles per hour on the freeway. These bits of information are important, for they help children eventually integrate their knowledge of numbers into a measurement system.

Suggestions for Parents

On *Sesame Street,* Count Count has a love affair with numbers. Preschool children share the Count's love of numbers when counting is made a part of everyday experience. Perhaps the most common example is counting food. Here are a few of the many possibilities.

Children enjoy counting out the number of food treats they get to eat on a given occasion, such as nine M&Ms, twelve potato chips, or fourteen mini-marshmallows. By the same token, it is easier to cope with foods that are not favorites if children are encouraged to count the bites. "How many bites of meat are left on your plate?" Jeremy's dad wondered. "Six," Jeremy estimated. "I'll guess seven," his dad answered, and the challenge was on. By eating the meat in six bites, Jeremy could prove his father wrong. Preschool children like to count their food after cutting it into pieces. A single slice of cheese turns into

two pieces, then three, then four, five, and so on. The excitement of cutting is combined with the illusion that the food is expanding.

A second kind of everyday activity that is rich in counting possibilities is physical movement. Counting as you move encourages children to develop a steady counting rhythm and helps them learn the principle of one-to-one correspondence. Plan a family exercise time and count as you do your exercise. Count and jump, count and hop, count and clap. Count the number of times you bat a balloon back and forth, or count ten strokes as you and your child brush your teeth. A game of "drop and count" will demonstrate that each item gets counted once and only once. Count pennies as your child drops them in a piggy bank, or count blocks as you drop them into a box.

There are opportunities to count any collection of objects that a preschool child values: a set of miniature race cars, a bedful of stuffed animals, a bucket of seashells. If your child counts easily to twenty or thirty, you might introduce the idea of counting by twos. Arrange the collection in two parallel lines in order to demonstrate the logic of two, four, six, eight. Advanced counters are interested in counting by tens. Dimes are an ideal choice for teaching this concept: 10 cents, 20 cents, 30 cents . . . a dollar.

Another activity that allows children to practice their number skills is making a counting book. You and your child can glue pictures or small objects (like buttons, leaves, cotton balls) on pieces of paper and then bind the pages together in a notebook. A counting book may consist of various sets that represent the same number, such as a "Book of 6" with six objects per page. Magazines, newspapers, and shopping catalogs are full of pictures that show naturally occurring sets. Or a counting book may challenge children to count objects in different configurations: in a circular pattern, a square, a cross, a star, and so forth. When counting these collections, or in any other counting activity, your emphasis should be on teaching the idea of one-to-one correspondence, not on total accuracy. The important accomplishment is learning that one number goes with each object.

Counting is more enjoyable when it is shared with someone else. Counting can be social, and the skill develops naturally as children join in and imitate their parents. Counting objects together will help your child learn the correct number sequence. In addition you can introduce finger games, songs, and activities that reinforce rote counting. Trips in the car are an excellent time for singing number songs like "Ten Little Indians" or "This Old Man." If you are a passenger in the car, you might try a simple rhythm game. Alternate slapping your thighs and clapping your hands, while counting as you clap. You can adjust the game to your child's ability: slowing down or speeding up the rhythm, counting by ones, twos, or tens. It's also fun to count backward. Counting backward helps children get a feeling for the idea that mathematical operations are reversible, that numbers form a unified system.

As children become familiar with the names of numbers, they are likely to notice numerals in their environment: digital clocks, telephones, price tags, and calendars. Once you notice what numerals attract your child, you can help extend this interest. Again, there are simple games that reinforce numeral recognition. Card games are a prime example. A good game to start with is a version of Snap. Place the deck face down, then turn over the top card and lay it face up on the table. Ask your child to turn over another card. Continue taking turns in this way, picking up pairs whenever two matching cards are face up. Another numeral recognition game that can be adapted for preschool children is Bingo. Use a smaller matrix ($3'' \times 3''$ or $4'' \times 4''$) and color code the columns. The first column might be blue and numbered from one to ten; the second column red with numbers from eleven to twenty, and so on. Using the colors helps your child locate the correct column, and reducing the matrix speeds up the game.

If you feel your child is ready for addition and subtraction, experiment with one of the following games. Show your child that you have two or three pennies in your hand. Then close your hand and place one more penny into your closed

fist, saying "I started with three pennies and I added one more; how many do you think I have now?" As soon as your child gives an answer, open your hand and let him count the pennies. If the child is wrong, see if he wants to play again. The idea is to treat the activity as a magic trick, one in which the child can outwit the magician by giving the correct number of hidden pennies.

An alternative game involves guessing "how many are missing?":

Mother: Okay, Gretchen, see how many shells I have lined up?

Gretchen: One, two, three, four, five.

Mother: Right. Now close your eyes. I'm going to take some away. Okay, open your eyes—how many do you think I took away?

Gretchen (Counting the holes that are left in the line of shells): I know, you took two shells.

A third possibility is to illustrate sums with the fingers on both hands:

Simon Says:	Hold up eight fingers.
	Good, that's four and four.
Now, Simon Says:	Make eight a different way—it can't be four and four.
	Let's try five . . . and three, good.
Now, Simon Says:	Hold up six fingers. . . .

Children who show interest in these addition and subtraction games will enjoy story problems even more. Mental arithmetic gains appeal when it is presented in the context of a real problem:

We invited eight children to your party and we have only five favors. How many more favors do we need to buy at the store?

With you and your sister and me, we are taking up three seatbelts. We have five seatbelts in the car altogether. How many more children can we put in the car with everyone still having a seatbelt?

Even in the case of children who are mathematically advanced, parents need to go slowly with calculation problems. A child's newly created system of double counting can easily be overwhelmed. Accuracy is less important than practicing the process. Young children can be taught to memorize certain number facts, but it is the double-counting process that enables them to understand the logic of addition and subtraction. Being able to figure out an answer in your head, even if it is not always accurate, is an exciting accomplishment. By maintaining a playful and supportive approach to mathematics, parents can help children advance toward this goal at their own pace.

As we look at the many different concepts involved in an elementary understanding of numbers, the wonder is that preschool children can learn so much so quickly. Children seem to have a natural affinity for numbers. Counting fingers and toes, reciting number rhymes, repeating finger games, counting out cookies, arranging collections into sets, and completing number puzzles are play activities that children really enjoy. As long as we help each child pursue counting in his own way, number learning will be seen as a game to play and a skill to master.

Part V
PLAYING WITH FRIENDS

Jenna: Guess what happened at school today?

Mom: What happened?

Jenna: Adam held my hand when we did our exercises!

Making friends is the crowning achievement of the preschool years. From the point of view of the preschool child, the epitome of having a good time is playing with a friend. Some theorists describe peer attraction on the basis of self-assessment. Their claim is that children get a realistic estimate of their own strengths and weaknesses by comparing themselves with their peers. Other theorists describe friendmaking in more dynamic terms. As peers play together, they learn to make adjustments, compromise, and co-construct the rules of their games and the terms of their friendship. But whatever the rationale, the importance of friendship in the preschool years cannot be overestimated.

Section V, "Play with Friends," is divided into three chapters. In Chapter 11, "Imaginary Friends," we describe how children use dolls, stuffed animals and make-believe friends as substitutes for real friends. In Chapter 12, "Intimate Friends," we look at the basis of friend selection and describe the interactions of close and long-term friends. In Chapter 13, "Group Play," our focus is on both group and one-on-one play. We identify different leadership and followership styles and describe the kinds of social skills that children acquire in the preschool setting.

In the final section of each chapter, we look at ways in which parents can encourage and support their own children's friendship-building skills.

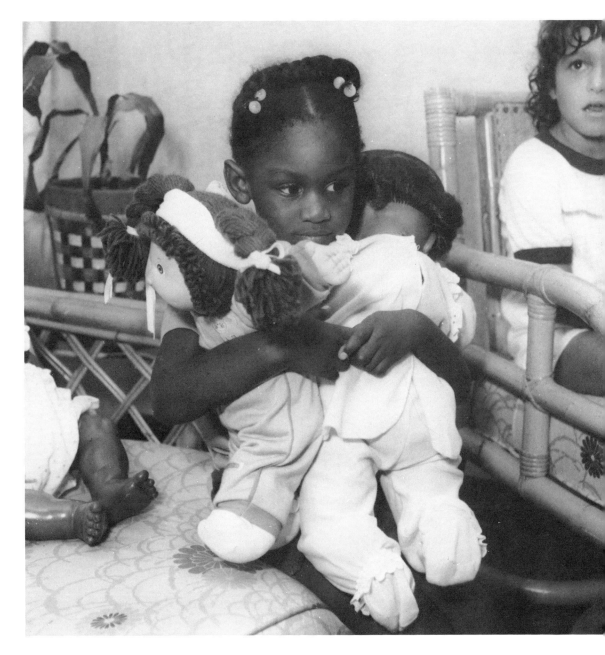

Here's Tom Thumb,
  Little fellow come,
Dance between my fingers.
  Rum-tum-tum.
Mind your little steps,
  Mind you never fail
To take a spring and jump
  Over my thumbnail.

Children demonstrate a natural bent for creating nonhuman companions. Among infants and toddlers, these companions range from traditional dolls and stuffed animals to inanimate objects like blankets and bottles. In fact, very young children may form an attachment with virtually any object that makes them feel secure.

By the beginning of the preschool period, imaginary companions have become more than security objects. Now they have personalities and lifelike characteristics, and their role includes helping children act out wishes on a fantasy level. In this chapter, we look at different ways in which preschool children create imaginary companions. Sometimes they are babies who need to be nurtured, sometimes they are peers who like to play, and sometimes they are older, more powerful confidantes. In all of these forms, imaginary companions represent an important first step in the process of making friends.

From Baby Friends to Peer Friends

The imaginary companions of young preschoolers are most often babies. Favorite babies may be either dolls or stuffed animals. New dolls and stuffed animals are seldom accepted as babies without an appropriate breaking-in period. Softness, floppiness, big eyes, and a sad expression seem to facilitate the adoption process.

Many children adopt an imaginary baby and begin care-giving before they reach preschool age. This play, however, tends to be highly repetitive and mechanical. The doll is fed, burped, and fed again. Or, if the child has a younger sibling in the house, he may add diaper changing to the routine. Again, as soon

as the doll's bottom is wiped and a facsimile of a diaper put on, it is time for another diaper change.

During the preschool years, care-giver play becomes less repetitive and goes beyond simple imitation. The children actually assume the role of parent and create a parent-child relationship with their dolls. Play becomes highly conversational; children learn to change their voices, depending on whether they are talking to the doll or for the doll. In their role as parents, the children relish decision making, deciding what to do when the baby gets sick or acts naughty or is old enough to celebrate a birthday.

Most significantly, the imaginary babies take on the characteristics of the children who are pretending to be their parents. The children create another version of themselves by projecting their own image on to make-believe babies. As the doll babies mirror the wishes and fears of the children, they become companions, for it is easy to make friends with someone who is just like you.

"Velvet needs money in her pockets," Laura explained to her mother as she prepared to take her favorite doll on a shopping trip. Arriving home later, Laura told her mother that it was time for Laura to take a nap. As she tucked Velvet into bed, she gave her some toys to play with—a Donald Duck doll, a pocketbook, a nail file, a ring, and a bracelet—just the sort of things that Laura liked to play with in her own bed.

When a baby doll graduates to the role of peer, there is a subtle shift in the language that accompanies pretending. Instead of talking about what needs to be done to take care of the baby, children talk about the doll's feelings and ideas. Alyse, Kori's baby doll, aged several years overnight and began looking forward to her fourth birthday. As Kori explained to her mother:

> Alyse will be four on her birthday. She just drinks bottles at night. Oh, Alyse, what's wrong? Wait just a minute. I'll get your bottle. Don't cry, you shouldn't do that.

From Peer Friend to Superfriend

For some children, favorite imaginary companions remain peers throughout the preschool years. These dolls and stuffed animals participate in whatever the children do. If the child gets dressed up in fancy clothes, so does the doll. If the child packs a bag for an overnight stay at Grandma's, the doll needs to pack a bag too. The imaginary companions even shadow children when they act out pretend themes. "I'm a policeman," Brandon announced to his parents, "and this is Garfield, the police cat." Later Brandon changed to a cowboy, and Garfield followed suit as a "cowboy cat."

With the loyalty of a younger friend, these companions are always willing to play the role of "extra." A child who plays doctor can count on them to be patients. A child who wants to be a teacher has a ready-made classroom of pupils. Jackie used her imaginary companions for a church service. With a pillow on the floor as the first-row pew, Jackie lined up her dolls and solemnly began the service. "Jesus loves you," she intoned in a deep sonorous voice, holding a Bible upside down. "Jesus wants you to go to heaven. Did you all bring your lesson books today? Turn to page eighty-four. Now—everybody together —sing. Jesus is on the water."

As preschool children become more sophisticated about the world beyond their immediate family and everyday experiences, the nature of their imaginary companions can change. Rather suddenly, baby dolls are replaced by more sophisticated mass-produced toys such as Care Bears, My Little Ponies, Strawberry Shortcake dolls, Get-Along Gang dolls, and Barbies. Stuffed animals are displaced by superhero dolls, Star Wars figures, gobots, and deceptagons. Although the children may have played with these various dolls earlier, they now assume a new importance in the children's play.

Clearly such imaginary companions are created and marketed through the mass media, particularly television. Their rise to prominence suggests that children are substituting the fantasy themes of television for the earlier themes

that grew out of their personal experience. It also suggests that the media producers have struck a responsive chord in preschool children.

As we speculate on the basis of the appeal of these media-created characters, we are struck by the fact that boys and girls select different favorites. Girls are especially attracted to teenage dolls that come with an extensive wardrobe. Boys are attracted to robots and action figures that are fearless, reckless, heroic, or malevolent.

The prototype of adolescent glamour dolls is Barbie, an unchallenged favorite since the middle '50s. In contrast to doll companions that take on the personality of their owner, Barbie comes with a ready-made personality of her own. As children sort out Barbie's wardrobe, fix up her dressing table, or prepare her for a dance, they are projecting themselves into a fantasy role. In a

sense, Barbie, with her fancy clothes and expensive possessions, is a modern Cinderella.

While preschool girls use Barbie dolls as the basis of their director-producer-type pretending, the pretend play of preschool boys is most frequently linked to television fantasies. Collections of miniature robots and superheroes become their treasured possessions. These various characters and vehicles are imbued with magic power that can keep a preschooler safe.

Hans had amassed an impressive collection of robots, which were his constant companions. One day after a boat trip with his parents, Hans discovered that he had left his favorite robot, Bumblebee, on the boat. Hans was completely distraught by this discovery. After two days of listening to his son lament, Hans's father finally went back to the boat to retrieve the tiny toy.

Although miniature objects may serve as protectors, these toys are used most frequently as props for director-producer-type pretending. Kevin, at five years old, turned his bathtub into an outer-space combat zone:

> "*Vrroom - vrooom - swish - swish - tuush - tuush - zp - u - zp*—Here he comes. Flying through the air. Man the space gun. Four-two-one blast off! *Tat-a-tat-tat-a-tat.* Watch out from above. We're under attack!"

Some parents express concerns about media-inspired pretending. Are girls who play with Barbie dolls buying into superficial and materialistic values? Are boys who play with robots obsessed with death and violence? While these concerns are legitimate, parents should realize that this type of play serves a useful purpose. One of the functions of pretend play is to come to terms with situations that are confusing or unfamiliar. Children in our culture are exposed to sexual and violent themes despite parental efforts to shield them. Pretend play can be thought of as a safety valve, allowing children to explore mature social roles and other scary facets of the grown-up world at a safe distance.

Invisible Friends

Nicholas: There it is Daddy. Right there it is. That's Dooka-Doo's House.

Daddy: Good, let's go in and visit.

Nicholas: Dooka-Doo is shopping at the mall.

Invisible friends like Dooka-Doo are often invented by three-year-olds who have limited access to real friends. These invisible friends can be puzzling. Parents often claim that they don't know if their child really believes in the existence of the pretend friend or whether these companions are just a device for spoofing parents and getting adult attention. At times, children really seem to believe in their invisible friends—when sharing a secret, issuing a command, or protecting the friend from a parent who is about to sit in his or her special chair. At other times, children seem to be quite aware that their friend is an invention.

When Michelle blamed Mouchie for a wet spot in the bed, Michelle's parents detected a guilty smile. When Nicholas claimed that he couldn't go to school because Dooka-Doo would be lonesome, both father and son knew full well that Nicholas was hunting for an excuse to stay home.

Although invisible friends are often used as scapegoats or alibis, they serve other functions as well. For children who spend a lot of time by themselves, the imaginary friend may be a companion in a true sense, accompanying the child on make-believe excursions or serving as an audience when the child puts on a performance.

The names that children give their invisible friends are often suggestive of their function. Chris' after-school imaginary playmates were given the name of whomever sat beside him at school. Alexis called her invisible friend Ryan, the name of her favorite real friend. When Alexis was told that she couldn't have Ryan over, she explained to her mother that Ryan was only just pretend.

Quite commonly, the name given to an imaginary friend is a diminutive form or variation of the child's own name. Jad's imaginary playmate was called JaJa. Candice named her playmate Candy Cue. In these cases, the invisible friend may be a kind of alter ego, sharing the child's feelings and expressing the child's thoughts. When Jad was upset about not going to the soccer game with his Dad, JaJa was offered consolation. "You mad cause Daddy don't take you to the soccer game? Daddy take you next time."

Troy's imaginary friends were named John and Peter. They lived in the vestibule wall and made their appearance when Troy's parents were busy. Their assigned function was to listen while Troy described his business dealings.

"What a day!" he announced to his silent companions. "I sold sixteen sinks, fourteen ice makers, and twelve bar stools."

With few exceptions, children abandon their invisible friends between the ages of three-and-a-half and four. In most cases, the friends are simply forgotten, but occasionally the invisible friend suffers a tragic fate. Abbeba, who used to live in Abby's hall, died in an accident. Jan's friend, Noonie-No, jumped into the ocean and "drowned." No one really knows why children are so likely to "kill off" an invisible friend. It may be that children are communicating the message that their friend was only just pretend. We could also speculate that the killing off of an invisible friend is the child's way of exploring death and violence.

Suggestions for Parents

A child's "conversation" with an imaginary friend can tune parents in to his feelings. When a child comforts his doll on the way to the doctor, parents recognize that their child is scared. A helpful reaction is to talk to the doll, telling it that this is just a checkup or that the shot will be just a quick pinch. Just as the child is using the doll to communicate to his parents, parents can address the doll as a way of talking to their child. The special role that imaginary friends play in enhancing this kind of communication make them important members of the family.

Because dolls and stuffed animals are so special to young children, it is important for parents to treat these imaginary friends as honored members of the family. Try to remember their names and greet them when they appear on the scene. Make every effort to help your child find a missing doll, as the loss of a favorite friend can be traumatic. Statements like, "I warned you to leave it home," when your child is frantically searching for a missing stuffed animal can only make matters worse.

Be careful not to overload your child with dolls or stuffed animals. It is harder for children to build up close attachments when their family is too extensive. Identify your child's favorite dolls or stuffed animals and buy accessories for these favorites, such as pajamas, play clothes, blankets, strollers, brush and comb sets, or a set of miniature dishes. When favorite dolls have their own special possessions, children are likely to imbue them with corresponding personality traits. (A teddy with a pair of blue jeans likes out-of-door play. A doll

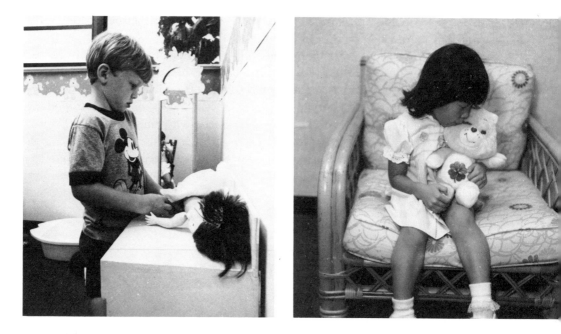

with a tea set enjoys having company.) As children develop personalities for their dolls, they enhance their value as companions.

Talk directly to your child's doll and assume the doll has feelings. This technique provides a means for reprimanding your child in a gentle way or for helping your child recognize and express his feelings.

Brenan was giving flying lessons to Garfield and, in the process, hit his sister on the head. Instead of scolding Brenan, his mother addressed her comments to Garfield:

> Garfield, you have not been a safe flyer. You are going to have to stay on top of the bureau until I give you permission to get down.

On another occasion, Brenan had a cold and was not allowed to go out to dinner. Before Brenan could express his disappointment through a temper tantrum, his mother began a conversation with Garfield:

> Garfield, I know how sad you are about not going out to the restaurant. But you know you have a cold and you want to be better by your birthday. Brenan has a cold, too. He is going to stay home and take good care of you. Good, Garfield, I'm proud of you. You are not even crying.

Use an imaginary friend to role-play problematic situations. When Alexis put up a fuss about staying home with a baby-sitter, her mother took out Alexis' older sister's doll. "You know what? Peggy (the doll) is all upset. She doesn't want to stay in the room all by herself. Do you suppose you could take care of her until your sister comes home? Well, look at that. She feels better already." The strategy worked. Alexis was so pleased about being trusted with her sister's favorite doll that she forgot about her objections to the baby-sitter.

If your child has an invisible friend, go along with it. In actuality, invisible friends can spark playful conversations that you and your child can enjoy. Patricia had an invisible friend called Pattymouche who lived in the family car. On the way to play group in the morning, Patricia and her dad would tell silly stories to Pattymouche.

Sometimes parents worry about talking to their child's invisible friend. They see it as blurring for their child the distinction between real and pretend. This fear is groundless. Usually around four years old, children dismiss their invisible friends and turn their interest toward real ones.

Soon after her birthday, Patricia said to her mother, "My friend Pattymouche moved to Mount Washington."

As we look at the different ways that young children play with their nonhuman companions we see children building up the skills that are the basis for making friends. Attachments to dolls, stuffed animals and invisible friends give children genuine experiences with loving, caring, protecting, and sharing. At the same time, parents can benefit from a child's attachment to an imaginary friend. The friend helps the child reveal his or her feelings and provides a nonthreatening way to handle difficult situations, and to communicate values.

Chapter 12
INTIMATE FRIENDS

Oh jolly playmates
Come out and play with me
And bring your dollies three
Climb up my apple tree
Look down my rain barrel
Slide down my cellar door
And we'll be jolly friends
For evermore.

Bryce didn't sit beside me at school.
Bryce didn't let me bite his sandwich.
Bryce isn't even my best friend and he can't come to my birthday
    party.

Exchanging imaginary playmates for real playmates is not easy. Unlike imaginary playmates, real friends are not always available, and when they are available, they are not always in a good mood. Real friends have minds of their own. Sometimes they won't sit beside you, and sometimes they won't share their peanut-butter sandwiches. Nevertheless, once preschool children start to make friends with their peers, they become more and more oriented toward spending time with them.

For most preschool children, the bond they share with parents is their first experience with friendship. Peer friendship represents a new step; peer friends are essentially equal, while parent–child friendships are not. Having a peer friend requires perseverance and initiative. And in the process of making friends with each other, the children gain a new appreciation of what it means to cooperate and share.

Making Friends

During the preschool years, a friend is someone who will play with you and, by implication, someone who will share toys with you. Such friends are where you find them. Although preschool children show preferences for particular friends, friendship is more often a matter of convenience than selection. Children who live near each other, or who are brought together frequently for whatever reason, will generally become good friends.

Friendships between preschoolers easily cross sexual, racial, and age barriers. At school, Jimmy played primarily with boys as did most of the boys in his class. At home, however, his best friend was Beth, who lived two doors down the street. Jill's best friend, by contrast, was her cousin Amanda, even though Jill was five and Amanda only three.

The most intense and rewarding friendships seem to evolve within the context of an "extended family." This extended family may be of the traditional sort, in which the children of grown siblings have regular contact. Or it may be a situation in which several mothers who are good friends get together regularly with their children. In either event, the children become accustomed to visiting in each others' homes. Because their parents are usually present, these visits are seldom traumatic for the children and the end result is intimacy without tension. The children quite naturally become best friends.

An interesting characteristic of best friends is the ritualistic nature of their interaction. Reunions always seem to begin with the same play routine. Emily and Stacy had been companions since infancy. Their frequent reunions inevitably began with a happy exchange of nonsense words. "Let's go play goop-a-goop," suggested Emily. "Let's play goop-a-goop poo poo," added Stacy. At this point, the two girls burst into raucous and exaggerated laughter.

Repeating a well-established play routine, especially one that is silly, gives the friends a way to get started without planning or negotiating, and sets the mood for further play. As preschool children grow older, they are not as likely to be dependent on a greeting ritual. The children have established a pattern of relating to each other; the play is both more flexible and more mature.

Debbie and Melissa, at five years old, enjoyed dressing up at Debbie's house. Melissa readily accepted Debbie's suggestion that they play Snow White, and she had no objection when Debbie assigned the lead role to herself. Since there were no other desirable parts, Melissa was even willing to be Prince Charming. Together they lined up the stuffed animals as dwarfs. "For seven long years, the fair Snow White kept sleeping," Debbie intoned as she lay on the bed. "Then one day a prince came riding through the forest. (Melissa mounts the hobby horse.) Quick as a wink, the prince unmounts his horse." "Oops," Melissa mutters as the horse tips over on its side. Both girls laugh and the rehearsal begins again.

While preschool children are likely to develop an intimate relationship with only one or two close friends, brief short-term friendships are established easily and frequently. These friendships may also be characterized by intensity and can help children develop the social skills that cement long-lasting relationships. Brenan and Josh, who had never met before, were jumping around in a crowded motel swimming pool. Josh's mother was sitting on the deck and had restricted him to the shallow end. Brenan's mother was standing in somewhat deeper water watching her son practice jumping. "Watch me, I can do something silly," Josh called out to Brenan's mother. Brenan's mother admired Josh's first silly trick knowing that her son would get into the act. "I can do something even sillier," Brenan announced predictably. Brenan's mother moved aside, and the two boys started a game of one upmanship jumping. Noticing that her son's teeth were chattering, Josh's mother ordered him out of the pool.

"But I'm playing with my friend" Josh protested vehemently. "Invite him to play out of the pool," countered his mother. Josh turned to Brenan, "Do you like transformers?" As the two boys poured over a coloring book and shared ideas about the colors of a deceptagon, Josh turned to Brenan and asked, "What's your name?"

The ability to establish peer contact without a formal introduction is common in preschool children. It is a kind of nothing-ventured-nothing-gained philosophy. If Brenan had not responded to Josh's play initiation, neither boy would have had a playmate. The chance to interact with a peer, which so enlivens play, overcame any feelings of shyness they might have had.

Conflicts with Friends

Like most relationships, the friendships of preschool children often go through an initial honeymoon period. During this time, two friends may seem like each other's shadows. Whatever one child suggests, the other agrees to do. "Me too" is the watchword of the day. Imitative play is an effective way to communicate "I want to be your friend." At the same time, this imitative play involves a low level of organization that makes it easy to maintain.

In time, most early friendships become somewhat competitive. When two friends ride their trikes, they race to the end of the driveway. When they swing on the playground side by side, they argue about who is going higher.

Preschool friends may sound petty as they bicker back and forth. ("I made the biggest mudpie." "My socks come up higher than your socks.") The children, in these instances, are using their friendship to further their self-definition. Competition serves to highlight each child's individuality. When Kenneth's grandmother remarked about how fast he could run, Kenneth replied matter-of-factly, "I'm the tallest boy in my class, but I'm only the second to fastest runner."

If peers serve as a standard for comparison, they also can provide support when children feel they are falling short. Jason was aware that he was less coordinated than many children his age. One day, at a birthday party, everyone was jumping on a rocking toy shaped like a banana. Jason finally decided to try it. At the last moment, however, he lost his nerve and began to cry. Later, when the other children were inside, Jason tried again with his friend, Alexis. In this

more private setting, with the help of a friend he succeeded in making the jump and excitedly called his mother to watch.

It takes time to learn how friendship is compatible with competition. A beginning point is recognizing that different activities work better with different friends. Adam, at three years old, already varied his play according to his play partner. When his next-door neighbor, Jeffrey, came over he would invite him to jump in the mud puddles. When four-year-old Patricia came over, he went on an ant hunt. When his school friend, Bertram, came over they went up to his room to play robots.

Older preschool children are able, at least some of the time, to avoid a conflict by planning cooperatively. Instead of fighting over competing ideas, they negotiate a compromise that allows for shared leadership:

Matthew:　Let's make a space station for my gobots.

Harold:　No, first I got to fix up skymaster. Watch out—here I come. *Crrt-u-crrr vrum vrum* out of my way!

Matthew:　No, Skymaster can't fly yet. He's out of space fuel. He needs to fill up with space fuel. Quick, we gotta build a space station with a fueling tank.

Harold:　You make the space station—I make the fool tank.

In practice, compromise is not always a pretty thing to watch, but progress does take place. At the beginning of the preschool period, children who are competing, whether it be for toys, play space, or recognition, often attack each other physically. The fight may range from a mild tug-of-war to an outright fistfight. By the end of the preschool period, most children, at least initially, try to solve conflict on a verbal level. Their instinct may still be to attack, but as long as the fight is limited to verbal aggression, the chances for a compromise are greater. After trading insults and playing independently for a few moments, it is not unusual to see the children drifting back together.

The most serious conflicts occur when children feel excluded by their friends. To be left out of peer play is a great insult, for friendship among preschoolers means playing together. Additional hurt comes when a child feels his or her friend now prefers to play with someone else. Feelings of jealousy run surprisingly deep.

Exclusion results more from the limited social understanding and skills of preschool children than from intentional cruelty. Two children playing together are not adept at including a third party, even if they have no real

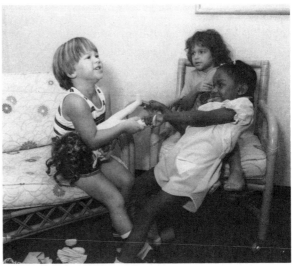

objections. "When Terry is playing with Solomon," Terry's mother told us, "he doesn't know what to do if Nicole knocks on the door. At first, he just stares as if struck dumb by her presence. Then, when she asks to play, he shouts 'No!' and slams the door shut. I don't think he is angry with Nicole; he just doesn't know how to cope with the situation."

The more complex relationships between three friends are hard to grasp. "Julie's not my friend anymore 'cause she plays with Andrew," Eric complained to his mother. Like other preschool children, Eric could not see beyond the idea of two-person friendship. He could be friends with Julie or friends with Andrew, but if Julie and Andrew became friends, he felt automatically left out. The possibility of three mutual friends eluded him.

Losing Friends

Friends can be lost through misunderstanding and disagreement. Preschool children do not usually have this problem, however. Although they are not skilled at making up after a quarrel, they are equally poor at staying mad. After a brief separation, friends who have argued begin to play again, and both appear to have forgotten that an argument ever occurred.

Preschool children do experience long-term anguish when a good friend moves away or dies. Jason's best friend, Harry, moved to Boston. Jason's questions about Harry give us a real sense of a child experiencing grief: "Where is Harry right now?" "What does it look like in Boston?" "Does Harry have any other friends who come to his house?" "Can we write a letter to Harry?" At the party for his fourth birthday, Jason insisted upon setting a place for Harry with a full complement of party favors.

The powerful effect of losing a friend underscores the intensity of many friendships that are formed during the preschool years. Children have much to learn about friendship, yet they are already able to achieve a meaningful kind of intimacy. Often they cannot describe this intimacy in words, but it is a formative experience. A considerable number of adults maintain contact with the friends they made during the preschool years.

Friendship with Adults

While the intimate friends of preschool children are most likely to be peers, it is not unusual for a preschool child to develop a close friendship with an adult who is not his or her parent. The special quality of this type of adult friendship stems from the fact that the adult has the opportunity to play at being a child. The fact that both parties recognize the pretext does not detract from the fun. As we listen in on the conversation of three-year-old Nicholas and his Aunt Patti, we can catch the flavor of their special relationship:

Aunt Patti: I'd like some orange juice. Would you squeeze me some orange juice, please.

Nicholas (Picking up an orange block):   Here's your orange juice. I made it.

Aunt Patti: Watch out for the seeds. You better strain my orange juice. The seeds make me choke.

Nicholas: I already strained it.

Aunt Patti: Great, now we can plant the seeds and grow an orange tree. There, I planted one. Would you water it, please?

Nicholas: Okay.

Aunt Patti: But what did you do with the rind?

Nicholas: What's a rind?

Aunt Patti: The outside part. We have to dip it in chocolate to make candy.

Suggestions for Parents

Recognizing the importance of friend making, most parents of preschool children play an active role in the development of their child's social skills. The way in which they intervene and the social skills they stress depend both on the characteristics of their child and on their own value system. In some families, a major concern is to help children develop the traits that will make them good

friends. In other families, parents are concerned with helping children be assertive and/or popular.

For parents who are concerned with their child's friendship skills, sharing toys can be a major issue. Second or third children learn by necessity about sharing, but for the first or only child, learning to share is a slow and difficult process. Children regard their toys as an extension of themselves and as a way of affirming their importance. The more stuffed animals they have, or the more crayons with points, the more important they feel they are. The visiting child who plays with their toys is violating their rights.

In order to make sharing easier for your child:

> Help your child prepare for a friend's visit by putting away the toys that he does not want to share.

· Assure your child that sharing a toy with a friend does not mean that the child can take the toy home.

· Help your child choose as "share toys," ones that will not break or get used up.

· Buy or collect toys for your child that are especially good for sharing such as construction sets, imaginative play materials, and large outdoor play equipment.

· Model sharing in your everyday interactions with your child. "This roll is delicious. Would you like me to share it with you?"

· Give your child opportunities to share. "I would really like a taste of your watermelon sherbet. Thank you for being such a good sharer."

· Play games with your child that involve taking turns.

While the techniques that we have listed may help your child overcome an initial reluctance to share toys, the problem of sharing disappears almost entirely when children engage peers in imaginative play. When they play out a theme, sharing the props is a natural part of the play. Helping children gather up props for a pretend theme in anticipation of a friend's visit is one of the most effective ways to reduce conflicts over sharing.

While parents of young preschool children are apt to be concerned about their child's learning to share, parents of older preschool children may be more concerned about their extremes of assertiveness. Some children are naturally assertive and will win their way in a conflict even if it requires shoving, shouting, pushing, or hitting. Other children are just the opposite. They handle a conflict situation by running away, ignoring it, or crying to an adult for help.

Parents differ in how assertive they would like their children to be, and no parent is happy with a child on either end of the continuum. If you feel that your child falls on the bully end of the continuum, you may want to invite slightly older children over to play. Plan an activity that will minimize opportunities for conflict such as putting together puzzles, pasting collages, or rolling out Play-Doh. After the play session, talk about how much fun it was and how nicely your child shared. Build up gradually to longer play sessions with your child in charge of the planning.

While some children fall on the overassertive side of the continuum, other children tend to be too passive. One way to deal with the situation is to teach the passive child how to protect him or herself with strong words.

"Let go of that toy. I had it first." "Stop pulling my hair. It hurts and I don't like it." It is also a good idea to help your child realize the importance of not overreacting. When a victim cries and screams, the bully-type child is more likely to "strike" again.

Another way to help the child who is too passive is to arrange opportunities for quiet play with a slightly younger friend. The confidence your child will gain with a younger friend will carry over into other situations with peers.

One of the most effective ways to help children develop appropriate social skills is to read stories about friendship. Stories about fictional animals who have difficulties with their friends are certainly easy to find. If you like to tell stories, you may want to arrange an imaginary conflict between your child's dolls or stuffed animals. Perhaps the Cabbage Patch doll could bully the teddy bear, and you and your child could find a good way to solve the problem.

As we look at the friend-making capacity of preschool children, we realize that the development of intimate friendships is one of the most critical tasks to face the preschool child. As children engage in sustained play with a peer, they are able to recognize and measure their own capabilities. At the same time, they are learning about sharing, compromising, and fairness, and are finding out ways to promote play ideas. Most importantly, they are learning about their own need and capacity for friendship.

Chapter 13
GROUP PLAY

Georgie Porgie, pudding and pie
Kissed the girls and made them cry;
When the boys came out to play,
Georgie Porgie ran away.

Gina: Want to hold my hand? We're friends, aren't we?

Mavilya: Yeah, we're friends cause we got purple jellies on.

Gina: Let's be friends all day and even after school.

For most preschool children, going to school is a happy and exhilarating experience. It is an opportunity to try out new toys, to paint, paste, and color, and to practice grown-up skills like counting and naming letters. Above all, preschool is the place where you play with other children and make friends.

Gaining Acceptance

Although most children would agree that playing with other children is the primary purpose of going to preschool, early efforts at making friends may not be successful. As we watch a young three-year-old attempting to gain entry into a preschool group, we realize how difficult it can be. Charlene, who has been in school for two days, tentatively approaches the sandbox where three girls are cooking dinner. "Can I make dinner, too?" "No," one of the girls replies. "Go away. We don't want you."

The way children react to an initial rebuff is a good indication of how quickly they will gain acceptance in the group. Some children walk away from the situation and either play by themselves or seek out the teacher. Other children force the issue even risking a hit or a shove. Still other children gradually and unobtrusively make their way into the group. Charlene chose the third alternative. She walked around the sandbox for a while and then edged up to the far end. After mixing and patting the sand around for a few minutes, she offered a sandcake to one of the children. The cake was accepted graciously and Charlene became part of the group.

Sooner or later, with few or many rebuffs, most preschool children are accepted into a peer group. Preschool peer groups tend to be small (three to five children) and relatively stable. The group is likely to be organized around a central pair with one child as leader and the other as selected follower. Often these groups have a dominance hierarchy with a nonassertive child at the bottom and the leader at the top.

Developing a Social Style

In most preschool classrooms, there are different types of leader and follower roles available depending on the organization of group play. The most common, and certainly the most visible, leader type is the director of a pretend family. Ordinarily, the director takes the part of mother. As mother of the family, she selects the space in which to play and controls the props. The roles of big sister, big brother, husband, or baby are assigned to her faithful followers. As we watch these directors in action, two aspects of their behavior stand out. First, they are very verbal children who are skilled in giving orders. Second, they are so busy giving out orders that they are probably not having much fun.

Although mother of a family is a favorite role, preschool directors play a variety of prestigious roles that command the respect of their underlings. Fa-

vorite roles include doctor, police chief, and superhero. Here is director, Walter, playing the role of paramedic:

> Walter: Get the bandage. Get the needles; can't you see he's bleeding. No—not that one—its too small. Hurry, man, we need medicine, we need pills. Who has the Band-Aids? We got to operate! Hold him down! He's wiggling!
>
> Charles: Here, I got you a knife. Does he need sleeping stuff?

A second preschool leadership type is the teacher-helper. In contrast to directors, who surround themselves with a group of faithful followers, the teacher-helper child enjoys intimate play with one or two other children. The salient characteristic of the teacher-helper is their reliance on reason and persuasion and their ability to moderate quarrels:

> Eric: I want to be the cashier.
>
> Peter: No, you were last time. It's my turn.
>
> Andrew (A teacher-helper): This store is big. It needs two cashiers.

Another leadership style that is seen somewhat less frequently in the preschool classroom is the "monarch." Their style is distinctly different from either the director or the teacher-helper. Monarchs, who are the leaders of large casual groups, are more interested in entertaining than in getting their ideas accepted. They are good-natured, self-confident, and full of play ideas. Their goal is to have a good time. Although they may get loud and boisterous, their intensions are never aggressive. Often, they are able to use their good spirits and sense of humor to turn a potential conflict into a harmless game.

A group of preschool children were collected on the playground quarreling over a Hula Hoop. The teacher was about to intervene when Carlos arrived on the scene and pulled the Hula Hoop out of everyone's hands. Seconds later, the group had turned into a train of wild circus animals leaping through the burning ring that "Carlos, the great ring master" was holding in the air.

An interesting characteristic of the three leader types is that each has a preferred kind of play. Teacher-helpers like intimate play where they can use their verbal skills to good advantage. Directors enjoy actor-type pretend play with around four to six players. With too few children, they can't exercise enough authority, and with too many, they might lose control. Monarchs, who are not at all concerned about keeping things under control, enjoy playing with

large groups. They love raucous rough-and-tumble play, and the more children who join the group, the better they like it.

Followers are likely to select a play group because they like the style of the leader. Although they are free to move from group to group, they gravitate most frequently to one particular group. The shyest followers enjoy intimate play with a teacher-helper as leader. Children who enjoy pretend play will select a medium-size group with a director as leader. Children who like more active wild play are likely to follow a monarch. Followers tend to be popular and satisfied with their social status.

Some preschool children do not fall into either follower or leader classification. First, there are the versatile children who are equally successful as leaders or followers. They are assertive enough to take the lead when they have a good play idea, and flexible enough to follow a leader when it appears desirable. Brooke was playing the part of big sister in a pretend family group with Courtney as director-mother. When Courtney was called away by the teacher, Brooke took over the director role. "It's all right, children: Mother will be back in a few minutes. We'll roll out the pancakes for dinner."

A second social style that cannot be classified as leader or follower is the vassal type. These children are subservient to a selected leader and bossy toward other children within the group. Because they are vulnerable from two sides, vassals are under a lot of stress. On one hand, their chosen leader could desert them and go off with another playmate. On the other hand, another underling could come along and take over the role of faithful servant. Vassals are likely to aggress against children who try to play up to their leader.

Assuming a leadership role in a preschool dominance hierarchy is not necessarily equated with social success or popularity. Some of the more popular children in a preschool are followers rather than leaders. Other children who are well liked by their peers have a flexible social style. Even children who play alone much of the time may be liked by the group. The children who are likely to face rejection are the bolder children who have difficulty with sharing and controlling their impulses or the insecure children who do a lot of whining and crying.

Learning to Play by the Rules

The opportunity to develop a social style and find a position within the social structure is an important outcome of the preschool experience. Another benefit is the opportunity to develop the skills for group games. Children at this age begin to use rules as a way of organizing play. A favorite game for three-year-olds is a version of follow the leader in which children take turns shouting out

rules and directives. "You got to jump with your hands on your head. See me? Do it this way." The unspoken rule for this kind of game is that children take turns making rules.

rules for preschool

With four- and five-year-olds, the games that children play together may have more complicated rules. A game may involve jumping off the second stair in a silly position or jumping over the poison rocks as you race around the playground. Children who violate a rule may be shouted at, but the game goes on with a full complement of players. Even though the rules of older preschoolers are more complex, they serve the same purpose as the rules of the younger preschooler. Children are eager to use rules because they find they are a way to keep the game going.

The concept of using rules to enhance competition or as a way of assuring fairness eludes preschool children. When preschoolers mimic the competitive games of older children, they are likely to use the rules to make themselves the winner. Here is Cynthia playing checkers with her doll:

> "Okay, Donna Kate, you get the black pieces and I get the red ones. Now it's my turn. I take the black pieces. Your turn. Good jump. I take the red pieces. This is a good game."

Suggestions for Parents

Although parents and children alike recognize the social value of a good pre-school experience, entering a preschool for the first time can be scary. The initial task that parents have is to select an appropriate preschool. The second task is to help your child separate from home and gain acceptance in the peer group.

There are many criteria that parents use in selecting a preschool, and it is always difficult to find a school that meets every criteria. For parents who place a high priority on social skills, it is important to seek out a preschool where this priority is shared. A school's concern with social development is reflected in the selection of teachers, the curriculum objectives, and the physical layout of the classroom and the playground.

The teacher plays a critical role in establishing a classroom climate where children play well together. An effective teacher maintains control without being restrictive. She sets classroom rules in advance to minimize the potential of conflict and intervenes in a nonpunitive way when a conflict arises. At the same time, she recognizes and values different social styles, helping children achieve success with their self-chosen style. Finally, an effective teacher models social skills in her respectful interactions with children, fellow staff, and parents.

The physical layout of the classroom and playground should reflect a concern with social-skill development. Small enclosed play spaces encourage intimate play, while housekeeping corners, play structures, and playhouses encourage the formation of family groups. The availability of an assortment of props facilitates cooperative pretending.

The curriculum of a preschool, like the physical layout, should reflect a concern for the development of social skills. Time should be set aside every day for both free and organized play. During free-play periods, the children should have the freedom to choose their own friends and find their own play spaces. During organized play, the teacher should take the lead in initiating group activities. As much as possible, these games and activities should promote cooperation rather than competition. In a running activity, for instance, the goal could be to run across the playground holding hands, rather than to win the race.

Once parents have selected an appropriate preschool for their child, the next goal may be to help their child separate from home with as little anxiety as possible. Some parents feel that the best method for handling the initial separation is to go "cold turkey." They drop their child off at preschool and, as quickly as they can manage it, exit from the scene. With this approach, children are likely to have severe crying spells for a couple of days and then be fine. A second approach is to stay with the child at school until the child is ready to say good-bye. This method cuts down on the crying, but the adjustment takes longer to accomplish.

Whether a parent chooses the cold-turkey or the slow-and-easy approach to leave-taking makes little difference in the long run. What does make a difference is the way that the parent manages the leave-taking process. Here are some guidelines suggested by experienced teachers:

- Tell your child when you are leaving.

- Kiss him or her good-bye in a matter-of-fact way without prolonging the kiss.

- Demonstrate your confidence in the teacher by a complimentary statement. For example, "It looks as if you have made plans for a fun day."

- Give your child a concrete way to know when you are coming back (such as "right after good-bye, circle") and be there exactly on time.

- Once you have said good-bye, do not turn around.

Once a child has overcome the separation problem, the next concern may well be peer acceptance. When children come home from preschool complaining that nobody wants to play with them, parents remember back to their own childhood and empathize with their children. Almost every child experiences some rejection before gaining group acceptance. We can't fully protect our children from these rejections, but we can provide some help. Again, here are some suggestions made by experienced teachers:

- Model friendliness for your child. Talk cheerfully to their friends and invite over friends of your own.

- Within reason, let your child dress like the others. The child who is wearing a dress when everyone else is wearing blue jeans or cutoffs is at a disadvantage.

- Don't keep asking your child whom he or she played with each day. You may be pressuring your child to make friends before he or she is ready.

- Whenever possible, arrange after-school exchange visits with other children. It is easier to make friends with one child at a time.

- Make sure your child gets to school on time. Latecomers are sometimes left out of the play.

- Help your child practice the social skills at home that are valued by the preschool group. These include sharing, initiating play ideas, giving compliments, and accepting play suggestions.

A final common worry that parents have is that their child will be a problem in school. One parent whose child was having a hard time described her communications from the teacher. "I can hear the teacher's voice before I even pick up the phone. 'Your Emily looks so sweet and gentle, but she keeps beating up on the other children.' "

Despite the best efforts of parents, some children take longer than others to learn the social conventions of preschool. Children who are used to being listened to at home may have difficulty with the noncompliance of their peers. Children who have treasured their possessions may have some problems with sharing. In these situations, the most effective rule of thumb is to avoid being defensive with the teacher. When you and your child's teacher recognize that you have a shared concern, it is easier to talk about solutions.

Whether the period of adjustment is short or long, preschool is the place where children learn to be a part of a group and how to initiate friendships and handle social rebuffs. It is the place where they learn to read social cues and conform to social mores, where they develop their own social style as leaders or as followers. Most important, in preschool, children develop long-lasting relationships with their peers and experience the fun and security of being a part of the group.

Chapter 14
THE UNIQUE CHILD

THE LITTLE ELF

I met a little Elf-man, once,
Down where the lilies blow.
I asked him why he was so small,
And why he didn't grow.
He slightly frowned, and with his eye
He looked me through and through.
"I'm quite as big for me," said he,
"As you are big for you."

—JOHN KENDRICK BANGS

Terry: I'm going to be a ghost for Halloween, a real scary ghost.

Denise: And I'm going to be a ghost too, really really scary!

Brenan: Well, I'm going to be a peanut-butter sandwich.

Throughout this book, we have looked at different modes of child play. In describing these different modes, our focus has been on identifying developmental trends that typify the preschool child. There is a built-in danger to this approach. A focus on typical behavior can overlook the sources of difference that make each child's play unique.

In this chapter, we turn our attention to some of the sources of difference in the play behavior of young children. The chapter is divided into three sections. The first section focuses on differences related to age and gender. The second section focuses on differences related to individual interest, temperament, and developmental status. The final section describes ways in which parents influence the play of their children through their own interests, values, and interactive style.

Age and Gender Differences in Children's Play

Expectedly, the play behavior of three-, four- and five-year-olds differs in many ways: preferred play mode, the themes the children are likely to play out, the complexity and skill level of their play, and the dimension of social interaction. These age-related differences are particularly evident in the way that children pretend.

Three-Year-Old Play

Okay, Skoo-Ba-Doo, do up your seat belt.

We on the way to Grandma's house.

Vruum, vruum, vruum.

Whoops, got to get some gas.

Glup-plup-glup. Stay put, Skoo-Ba-Doo. I can do this myself.

Whether they are building castles in the sand, serving their parents a make-believe breakfast, or riding a tricycle to the gas-pump tree, the pretend play of three-year-olds has certain characteristic features. Three-year-olds typically choose themes that are pleasurable and familiar: going on a trip, making dinner, going shopping, celebrating a birthday. They gather favorite props with more enthusiasm than discrimination. Rachel, for example, insisted on piling all her mother's shoes in a paper bag in preparation for a shopping trip. They replay the same episodes over and over again, with little attention to temporal order, as when Adam first blew out the candles and then baked the cake. If parents ask to join in the play, the three-year-old is delighted.

Four-Year-Old Play

Four-year-old pretend play is less rigid, repetitive, and predictable than three-year-old play. Gender differences start to appear in four-year-old play, dividing boys and girls in the themes and settings they choose.

Four-year old boys need to have space for their pretending. They enjoy playing in groups and are likely to choose themes that involve running around, chasing, and making noise. Often there is an unseen enemy that must be destroyed or captured or a terrible danger that must be averted. Adults are usually kept out of the play and have difficulty following its sequence.

In contrast to four-year-old boys, many four-year-old girls continue the exploration of familiar themes. They enjoy pretending in intimate groups and seek out small enclosed places to play out their ideas. They tend to elaborate on domestic themes and often become adept at acting out roles:

Veronica (Playing the part of mother): Sister, give the baby dinner.
I got to go to class.

Susan (The sister):   But, Mother—last night I gave her dinner and she spit.

Veronica: When I say to do something, you do it, and that's that.

Five-Year-Old Play

By five years of age, both boys and girls engage in more elaborate pretending. Boys frequently choose to elaborate on television themes. In a school setting, boys gather in groups, shouting out threats and directions, mimicking the voice and gestures of their favorite cartoon heroes. In a home setting, alone or with a playmate, boys tend to play with action figures and transformers. The boys put their gobots through their paces, construct play spaces, and describe the powers and prowess of miniature creatures with extravagant boasts.

The pretend play of five-year-old girls continues to revolve around family themes with much of the playtime devoted to planning. During the planning period, the girls discuss story scripts, assign roles, choose a setting, and gather appropriate props. Frequently, the planning stage is so elaborate that the play never gets underway.

Gender Differences in Children's Play

Caroline: I don't want to play with boys. They are too rough and they fight.

Mother: But Caroline, you love playing with your cousin, Terry. And what about your friend Nicky?

Caroline: Well, Terry and Nicky don't fight.

Researchers for years have been studying the differences between the play of boys and girls. In general, there is an agreement that preschoolers, beginning around four years of age, prefer to play with same-sex peers. They also agree that boys tend to be more physically active than girls and enjoy playing in larger, more free-flowing groups.

The jury is still undecided on the question of the basis of the differences in the way girls and boys play. Some researchers describe inborn differences in aggressive tendencies. Others point to differences in the way girls and boys are socialized. Still others claim that differences in aggression are more apparent than real. While boys are more likely to get into fights than girls, girls are likely to use words to express their aggression. One thing does appear to be true: Whatever a priori differences exist between the play behavior of boys and girls, these differences are exaggerated when children play in same-sex groups.

Individual Differences

Each child's play is shaped by many factors other than age and gender: inborn temperament, position in the family, individual interests, developmental status, and early play experiences. While a discussion of all of these factors is beyond the scope of this book, we would like to describe three sources of individual differences that are especially significant. These factors are individual temperament, early and persistent interests and developmental status.

Differences Related to Temperment

Jeremy was playing race horse with his grandfather. In the beginning, they were both having fun, but after riding Jeremy around the room on his back seven times, Grandpa was getting tired. "This horse needs a rest," Grandpa complained. "Why don't we go in the kitchen and get a snack?" "No, no, giddyup, horsy," Jeremy insisted, pulling on his Grandpa's leg. A game that started off as fun ended up with a tantrum.

A great deal of developmental literature has been devoted to individual differences in infant temperament. Many temperamental characteristics can be identified in the first month of life and frequently persist into childhood. A calm, easy-to-soothe, and difficult-to-arouse baby may become an easy-going preschooler. An active, intense, or easily aroused baby may become an excitable and strong-minded preschooler who requires skillful management. Unquestionably, temperamental characteristics influence the kind of play a child selects and enjoys. An active and excitable child like Jeremy naturally gravitates to active and exciting play. An inactive, slow-to-warm-up, and highly sensitive child avoids play situations that are fast paced and intense.

An awareness of the temperamental characteristics of your child can help you select play materials and plan play activities. Children who get excited very easily do better when their active play is structured and limited in time. Jeremy's grandfather might have avoided the temper tantrum if he had redirected the race-horse play before Jeremy had gotten so worked up. Parents with a child who is timid and slow to warm up can introduce new and exciting play experiences in a gradual, nonthreatening way.

Differences Related to Interests

Although interests are certainly not inborn, we often see children who develop a very early interest that dominates their play. Hans, for example, at four years old, had a special interest in animals. He was particularly fascinated by little animals that squirmed or flew around. Out-of-doors, Hans hunted for bugs and lizards. Inside the house, he watched the fish in the aquarium, played with snails and newts, or read books about bugs. The neighbor called him "little cucaracha."

Hans' fascination and feeling of kinship with small living things was revealed in his conversational play. One day his Mother heard him talking to himself. "I wish I could be a slug, so I could go out in the rain puddle. I wish I could be a caterpillar, so I could climb into the tree."

Hans may be exceptional in the intensity and early appearance of his special interest, but most preschool children go through phases when an interest is all consuming. Joey went through a period where he browsed through dinosaur books, painted dinosaur pictures, told stories about Dookie the Dinosaur that lived in his closet, and built a structure out of blocks to house his dinosaur collection.

Rachel went through a stage where she wanted to be like her brother, Kenneth. She took over his favorite doll, played with his robots, slept in his "boy" pajamas, and refused to wear dresses. When Kenneth brought a book home from first grade, Rachel sat herself in an overstuffed chair and pretended she was reading.

Parents who share a child's special interest seek out opportunities to introduce related ideas. Joey's father took him on weekly excursions to a natural science museum, where they "discovered" all kinds of prehistoric animals. On the other hand, when parents do not enjoy or approve of their child's special interest, there is a potential for conflict. In these situations, parents have to examine the source of their discomfort and try to find a compromise. Hans' mother felt squeamish about the creepy, crawly things that Hans kept bringing into the house. The compromise they reached was a terrarium. Rachel's mother recognized that Rachel would get over her fascination about being like her brother when she went to school and made friends with girls. What disturbed her was that Rachel always looked so messy. The compromise she reached was to let Rachel wear boy's clothes around the house, but when they went somewhere special, Rachel had to dress like a girl.

Differences in Developmental Status

During the preschool years, children are working on three very critical tasks. First, they are establishing their individuality. They see themselves as separate from their parents; they begin to make choices for themselves and solve their own problems. Secondly, preschool children are establishing their position in the peer group. They are learning ways of making friends, initiating play ideas, and participating in group play. Thirdly, preschool children are mastering a set of skills related to control and personal expression. They are learning how to control their bodies and develop athletic prowess, how to control their fearfulness and contain their feelings of aggression, how to extract meaning from the things they see, hear, and experience, and how to share these meanings using words, crayons, building blocks, music, and movement.

The child who plays crash-up with his miniature school bus may be working on separation and autonomy. The child who is bossing other children in the play group may be trying to balance autonomy with peer acceptance. The child who is boasting about how high she can jump may be concerned about the mastery of new skills. By placing behavior in the context of developmental tasks, parents can recognize the plus side of seemingly negative behavior. Then, instead of intervening at the first hint of "inappropriate" behavior, parents can give their children space to play out conflicts and work toward their developmental goals.

Suggestions for Parents

Each chapter of this book concludes with suggestions for parents. In these sections, we describe different ways to tune in to and extend the play interests of young children. In this section, we ask you to think about yourself as well as your child. What are the values you hold? What kind of play do you enjoy? When do you feel most playful?

In both direct and indirect ways, the values that parents hold influence the play of their children. Parents who are concerned about violence may decide not to buy their child a toy gun or encourage aggressive play. Parents who are interested in breaking down gender barriers may buy dolls for their boys and trucks for their girls. Parents who want their children to be athletic may enroll them in gym or swim classes. Parents who value academic achievement may put aside time on a daily basis to read and write with their children.

Despite the efforts of their parents, children often make choices in play that ignore their parents' wishes. The child who was denied a gun may make one

out of a Tinker Toy and fire it around the house. The girl with a toy box full of trucks and tools may ask for a makeup kit. When this sort of thing happens, parents should not be alarmed. Their children have heard the message, but now they are tuning in to the culture of the peer group. More importantly, we need to recognize that a child living in a harmonious home will not become violent by carrying a toy gun or sexist by owning a makeup kit.

In many situations, parental values correspond to their personal interests —although this is not always the case. A parent who enjoys outdoor sports may regret her own lack of versatility and encourage her child to sing and dance. Fortunately, children have an uncanny way of knowing what we really enjoy. When parents have a special hobby or interest, children pick up the enthusiasm and want to share in the fun. This sharing of a genuine interest is a meaningful legacy that we can give our children.

In every parent, there is an oasis of playfulness for a child to tap. For some of us, this playfulness is brought out by rough-and-tumble play, for others by building a sand castle or inventing an imaginative game. Whatever releases this wonderful playfulness, the outcome is delightful. For a few beautiful moments, we become children with our children.

Recommended Reading for Parents

In recent years an excellent series on child development has been published by Harvard University Press: The Developing Child Series. Each book looks at a different topic in depth, summarizing current thinking in a readable fashion and providing the reader with an extensive bibliography. Several books in the series with information on preschool children are:

de Villiers, Peter and Jill. *Early Language.*
Clarke-Stewart, Alison. *Daycare.*
Diggory, Sylvia Farnham. *Learning Disabilities.*
Dunn, Judy. *Sisters and Brothers.*
Garvey, Catherine. *Children's Talk.*
Garvey, Catherine. *Play.*
Goodnow, Jacqueline. *Children's Drawing.*
Greenfield, Patricia. *Mind and Media.*
Kempe, Ruth. *Child Abuse.*
Parke, Ross. *Fathers.*
Zubin, Rick. *Children's Friendships.*

Recommended Reading for Children

CONVERSATIONAL PLAY

Brown, Margaret W. *The Dead Bird* (Reading, Massachusetts: Addison Wesley, 1958).

De Paola, Tomie. *Nana Upstairs and Nana Downstairs* (New York: Putnam, 1973).

Eastman, Philip D. *Are You My Mother?* (New York: Random House, 1960).

Greenfield, Eloise. *Africa Dream* (John Day, 1977).

Girard, Linda. *You Were Born on Your Very First Birthday* (Niles, Illinois: Albert Whitman, 1983).

Sendak, Maurice. *Where the Wild Things Are* (New York: Harper & Row, 1963).

Viorst, Judith. *The Tenth Good Thing About Barney* (New York: Atheneum, 1975).

DISCOVERY PLAY

Carle, Eric. *The Very Hungry Caterpillar* (New York: Philomel Books, 1969).

Carr, Rachel E. *Be a Frog, a Bird or a Tree: Rachel Carr's Creative Yoga Exercises for Children* (New York: Doubleday, 1973).

Cartwright, Sally. *Water is Wet* (New York: Coward McCann and Geoghegan, 1973).

Heller, Ruth. *The Reason for a Flower* (New York: Putnam, 1983).

Keats, Ezra Jack. *The Snowy Day* (New York: Viking, 1962).

Krauss, Ruth. *The Carrot Seed* (New York: Harper & Row, 1945).

Rogin, Gilbert. *What Happens Next* (New York: Random House, 1971).

Showers, Paul. *The Listening Walk* (New York: Thomas Y. Crowell, 1961).

CREATIVE PLAY

Arbuthnot, May H. and Shelton L. Root. *Time for Poetry* (Glenview, Illinois: Scott, Foresman, 1968).

Breinburg, Petronella. *Doctor Shawn* (New York: Thomas Y. Crowell, 1975).

Mayer, Mercer. *There's a Nightmare in My Closet* (New York: Dial, 1968).

Milne, A.A. *When We Were Very Young* (New York: E. P. Dutton, 1961).

Merriam, Eve. *Blackberry Ink* (New York: Morrow Junior Books, 1985).

Silverstein, Shel. *Who Wants a Cheap Rhinocerous?* (New York: Macmillan, 1983).

Walter, Mildred P. *Brother to the Wind* (New York: Lothrop, Lee & Shepard, 1985).

PLAYING WITH LETTERS AND NUMBERS

Funk, Tom. *I Read Signs* (New York: Holiday House, 1962).

Hague, Kathleen. *Alphabears: An ABC Book* (New York: Holt, Rinehart & Winston, 1984).

Hoban, Tana. *Big Ones, Little Ones* (New York: Greenwillow, 1976).

Katz, Bobbi. *Ten Little Care Bears Counting Book* (New York: Random House 1983).

Milne, A.A. *Pooh's Counting Book* (New York: E. P. Dutton, 1982).

PLAYING WITH FRIENDS

Cohen, Miriam. *Will I Have a Friend* (New York: Macmillan, 1967).

Gomi, Taro. *Sharing* (San Francisco: Heian International, 1981).

Keats, Ezra Jack. *A Letter to Amy* (New York: Harper Junior Books, 1968).

Rosenberg, Maxine B. *My Friend Leslie: The Story of a Handicapped Child* (New York: Lothrop, Lee & Shepard, 1983).

Sarnoff, Jane. *That's Not Fair* (New York: Scribner, 1980).

Surowieiki, Sandra L. *Joshua's Day* (Lollipop Power, 1977).

Williams, Margery. *The Velveteen Rabbit* (New York: Doubleday, 1957).

INDEX

Parenting and Child Care Books Available from Newmarket Press

Baby Massage
Parent-Child Bonding Through Touching
by Amelia D. Auckett; Introduction by Eva Reich, M.D.

A fully illustrated, practical, time-tested approach to the ancient art of baby massage. Topics include: bonding and body contact; baby massage as an alternative to drugs; healing the effects of birth trauma; baby massage as an expression of love; and more. "For anyone concerned with the care and nurturing of infants"—*Bookmarks.* Includes 34 photos and drawings, bibliography, index. (128 pages, 5½ × 8¼; $6.95 paperback)

Lynda Madaras' Growing Up Guide for Girls
by Lynda Madaras with Area Madaras

For pre-teens and teens; an all-new companion workbook/journal to the *What's Happening to My Body? Book for Girls* to help girls further explore their changing bodies and their relationships with parents and friends; complete with quizzes, exercises, and space to record personal experiences. Includes drawings, photographs, bibliography. (256 pages, 7¼ × 9; $16.95 hardcover, $9.95 paperback)

The "What's Happening to My Body?" Book for Boys
A Growing Up Guide for Parents and Sons
by Lynda Madaras, with Dane Saavedra; foreword by Ralph I. Lopez, M.D.

Written with candor, humor, and clarity, here is the much-needed information on the special problems boys face during puberty, and includes chapters on: changing size and shape; hair, perspiration, pimples, and voice changes; the reproductive organs; sexuality; and much more. "Down-to-earth, conversational treatment of a topic that remains taboo in many families"—*Washington Post.* Includes 40 drawings, charts, and diagrams, bibliography, index. (240 pages; 5½ × 8¼; $14.95 hardcover, $9.95, paperback)

The "What's Happening to My Body?" Book for Girls
A Growing Up Guide for Parents and Daughters
by Lynda Madaras, with Area Madaras; forewords by Cynthia W. Cooke, M.D., and Ralph I. Lopez, M.D.

Selected as a "Best Book for Young Adults" by the American Library Association, this carefully researched book provides detailed explanations of what takes place in a girl's body as she grows up. Includes chapters on: changing size and shape; changes in the reproductive organs; menstruation; puberty in boys; and much more. Includes 42 drawings, charts and diagrams, bibliography, index. (208 pages, 5½ × 8¼; $15.95 hardcover, $8.95 paperback)

How Do We Tell the Children?
A Parents' Guide to Helping Children Understand and Cope When Someone Dies
by Dan Schaefer and Christine Lyons; foreword by David Peretz, M.D.

This valuable, commonsense book provides the straightforward language to help parents explain death to children from three-year-olds to teenagers, while including insights from numerous psychologists, educators, and clergy. Special features include a 16-page crisis-intervention guide to deal with situations such as accidents, AIDS, terminal illness, and suicide. "Parents need this clear, extremely readable guide...highly recommended"—*Library Journal*.(160 pages, 5¹/₂ x 8¹/₄; $14.95 hardcover)

Your Child At Play: Birth to One Year
Discovering the Senses and Learning About the World
by Marilyn Segal, Ph.D.

Focuses on the subtle developmental changes that take place in each of the first twelve months of life and features over 400 activities that parent and child can enjoy together during day-to-day routines. "Insightful, warm, and practical...expert knowledge that's a must for every parent" (T. Berry Brazelton, M.D., Boston Children's Hospital). Includes over 250 photos, bibliography. (288 pages, 7¹/₄ × 9; $15.95 hardcover, $9.95 paperback)

Your Child at Play: One to Two Years
Exploring, Daily Living, Learning, and Making Friends
by Marilyn Segal, Ph.D., and Don Adcock, Ph.D.

Contains hundreds of suggestions for creative play and for coping with everyday life with a toddler, including situations such as going out in public, toilet training, and sibling rivalry. "An excellent guide to the hows, whys, and what-to-dos of play...the toy and activity suggestions are creative and interesting"—*Publishers Weekly*. Includes over 300 photos, bibliography, index. (224 pages, 7¹/₄ × 9; $15.95 hardcover, $9.95 paperback)

Your Child at Play: Two to Three Years
Growing Up, Language, and the Imagination
by Marilyn Segal, Ph.D., and Don Adcock, Ph.D.

Provides vivid descriptions of how two-year-olds see themselves, learn language, learn to play imaginatively, get along with others and make friends, and explore what's around them, and uses specific situations to describe and advise on routine problems and concerns common to this age, especially that of self-definition. Includes over 175 photos, bibliography, index. (208 pages, 7¹/₄ × 9; $15.95 hardcover, $9.95 paperback)

Your Child at Play: Three to Five Years
Conversation, Creativity, and Learning Letters, Words, and Numbers
by Marilyn Segal, Ph.D., and Don Adcock, Ph.D.

Hundreds of practical, innovative ideas for encouraging and enjoying the world of the preschooler, with separate sections devoted to conversational play, discovery play, creative play, playing with letters and numbers, and playing with friends. Includes 100 photos, bibliography, index. (224 pages, 7¹/₄ × 9; $15.95 hardcover, $9.95 paperback)

"Your Child at Play" Starter Set
Paperback volumes, 1, 2, and 3 in a gift box set. ($29.85)

About the Authors

Marilyn Segal, Ph.D., a developmental psychologist specializing in early childhood, is professor of human development and director of the Family Center at Nova University in Fort Lauderdale, Florida. The mother of five children, she is the author of sixteen books, including *Making Friends, Just Pretending,* and the four-volume series *Your Child at Play.* She is also the creator of the nine-part television series "To Reach a Child."

Don Adcock, Ph.D., is an associate director of the Family Center, a developmental psychologist, and a professor of early childhood development at Metropolitan State Hospital in Denver, Colorado. He is the coauthor of several books with Dr. Segal.